CONVERGENCES

To the Source of Christian Mystery

HANS URS VON BALTHASAR

CONVERGENCES

To the Source of Christian Mystery

TRANSLATED BY E. A. NELSON

IGNATIUS PRESS   SAN FRANCISCO

Title of German original:
Einfaltungen: auf Wegen christlicher Einigung
© 1969 by Kösel Verlag GmbH and Co., Munich

Cover by Victoria Hoke

© 1983 Ignatius Press, San Francisco
ISBN 0–89870–032–9
Library of Congress Catalogue Number 83–081853
Printed in the United States of America

CONTENTS

ACKNOWLEDGMENTS

The works here assembled were first published in the following publications. In order to leave the texts unchanged, minor repetitions have not been corrected.

"The Unity of Theology and Spirituality": *Gregorianum*, Fall 1969.

"The Unity of Theological Sciences": *Hochland* 60 (Dec. 1968), 693–703.

"The Multiplicity of Biblical Theologies and the Spirit of Unity in the Church": *Freiburger Zeitschrift für Philosophie und Theologie* 15 (1968), 171–89.

"The Unity of Our Lives": *Schweizer Rundschau* (Dec. 1968), 642–49.

"Only If": previously unpublished.

TRANSLATOR'S NOTE

The German title of this book, *Einfaltungen*, is an example of Hans Urs von Balthasar's creativity and the flexibility of the German language. Father von Balthasar uses this word and the verb *einfalten* to indicate a movement of recentralization and convergence, a return of multiplicity into the unity that is its source—"in-folding" as the reverse of unfolding. There is also a relationship to the words *Einfalt* and *einfältig*, describing the simplicity of simpletons or children—the "little ones" to whom the mysteries of God's kingdom are revealed according to a Gospel passage quoted several times in these pages. *Einfaltung* and *einfalten* have been translated with various forms and combinations of "to simplify", "to integrate" and "to converge".

I want to thank Dr. Erasmo Leiva-Merikakis, who suggested the English title for the book and answered many questions about translation. And I owe a special debt of gratitude to Mr. Michael Waldstein, who edited the first draft of this translation and made it significantly more accurate and lucid. *Vergelt's Euch Gott*.

—E. A. N.

FOREWORD

Up until the baroque era, Christian thought basked in the inexhaustible capacity of biblical revelation to be unfolded; the more branches, twigs, and leaves could be developed from the old stem, the more alive its root seemed to show itself. The last century, that of Darwin, spoke readily and in high spirits of the "evolution of dogma", and meant by this an expansion of the "treasure of wisdom and knowledge" (Col 2:3) hidden in Christ—an expansion which is legitimate and even demanded by the subject. But the extensive element almost always weakens intensity; besides, the orientation towards the Many runs contrary to the direction which all the religious thought and endeavor of humanity has taken from the very beginning: out of multiplicity to the One, to the "one thing necessary". *Qui trop embrasse, mal étreint*, says an energetic proverb.

Today we are on the way back—so much so that in many places it looks like confused flight. To save the foundering ship, things are thrown overboard blindly and at random. It is thought that liberating unity is achieved by ridding oneself of superfluous amassed goods. Not only churches

are emptied out until they stand there naked and
bare—"O trees of life, O when winter-like?"—
but so too are dogmatics. And as a matter of fact,
not only worm-eaten baroque altars stand ready
to be torn down, but also decayed theologies,
which can be roused to life scarcely or not at
all—unless one were to possess the magic wand of
an Henri de Lubac or a Karl Rahner, men who
know how to awaken unhoped-for timely living
substance from what seemed to be dead. The one
who can do such things, however, must possess a
valid criterion for the discernment of spirits: What
may and should be given up, and what on the
other hand needs only a creative transformation in
order to show itself helpful and indispensable?
Such discerning requires a knowledge and experience of the unity from which all multiplicity
went forth, and into which it must again let itself
be integrated if it truly was an explication of the
One. Unity always remains judge over its own
fullness: what cannot be led back into it without
force becomes a wall instead of a window.

Today we must investigate in what way the
Christian wealth, without losses—such as a vanquished army leaves behind on the battlefield
—relates to its origin: to the ineffable poverty of
the divine, incarnate, crucified love. We draw
close together, near to the sources and beginnings,

in order to hear exactly the "Word that was in the beginning". We unite ourselves outwardly; the question is whether the grace will be given us to collect ourselves inwardly as well.

This will not work without earnest effort of thought. Dogmas which we now know only from the outside, as the "content of the faith", and which have mostly been presented to us as such in catechism and from the pulpit, we must try to see from within again: as the manifestation of the one, single, indivisible truth of God. Supposing that this truth has presented itself to us as the eternal love which surprises us and lays its claims on us temporal creatures: Will not the basic articulations of the so-called Christian "doctrine"—Trinity, Incarnation, Cross and Resurrection, Church and Eucharist—become the immediate radiations of the glowing core of this truth? How should God, the One and Absolute, be eternal love, if he were not triune? And how, if he did not prove this being love to the end in the Cross and Eucharist for the world, which he created out of love, and if he did not take the world up, in Church and Resurrection, into the eternally moved rest of the exchange of love? Dogmas must be nothing other than aspects of the love which manifests itself and yet remains mystery within revelation; if they are no longer this, then gnosis has triumphed over love, human reason has conquered God, and at this instant—first in theology, then in the Church, then in the world—God is "dead".

We integrate: not out of resignation, but to regain the origin. We are stranded on the sand-banks of rationalism; we feel our way back to the sheer rock of the *Mysterium*. The rationalist can no longer pray, only rationalize, and in the end only criticize. But he who can no longer pray is incapable even of beginning a dialogue with one of the world's religions, let alone of showing in this discussion that more truth, because more absolute love, is present in the Christian religion.

Today the Christian people (or what is left of it) is searching with a lamp for persons who radiate something of the light, something of nearness to the source. It has long since had enough of the modernities, lacking all religious instinct, which trumpet at it from the press, the radio, and often enough from the pulpit. It is sad because it is untended, and an all too justified fear torments it that the "one thing necessary" could be totally blocked off and made inaccessible by the "experts", or the many dilettantes and apostates who pose as such. Often these are poor wretches, who must shout so loud in order to justify to themselves their inner predicament of no longer being able to pray. And the people has a sharp ear for spiritual sour notes.

We integrate, returning to the center. First we will show that between Christian thought and life (theology and spirituality) there exists such a unity that each of them can have a proper truth only through the other and together with it. We will then show how within theology, which seems to dissolve into many and ever more numerous disciplines, the unity of dogma governs and directs all specializations. Then we will consider the dreadful multiplicity of churches and its pseudo-justification through the alleged variety of theologies already in the New Testament; and we will seek the path, the frequently covered and overgrown path, which opens ways back for the lost ones, the ones who have drawn apart from each other, who have clambered out into the branches. Finally, each person must think briefly about himself, and ask himself where the *point vierge*, the integrated simplicity of his own existence might lie.

For only the simple eye sees a radiance that comes from the infinite simplicity. "I offer you praise, O Father, Lord of heaven and earth, because what you have hidden from the learned and the clever you have revealed to the merest children."

THE UNITY OF THEOLOGY
AND SPIRITUALITY

One cannot say which of the two was first present
in the biblical view: that which was much later
named "theology" or that which even later received
the name "spirituality". The original situation,
which holds unchanged from the beginnings of
Israel's history to the latest writings in the New
Testament, is that twofold engagement, God's
with mankind and mankind's with God, which is
called "covenant". This twofold engagement rests
on God's unilateral initiative—formulated in his
call and his promise to Abraham (which, however,
immediately includes Abraham's being taken into
total service). As problematical as the category
"covenant" proves to be historically and socio-
logically, it still clearly expresses the original
situation, which is of importance here: union,
turning to each other, and, in the resulting inner
space, the possibility of a living relationship, the
exchange of understanding, of faithfulness and
love. These aspects are only outgrowths of one

and the same thing, to such an extent that *one* word suffices to embrace them all: *emet*, *sedek*, *chesed*, among others, are "concepts of the totality"; they express what is and what ought to be—truth and proven reliability as well as truthfulness and trustworthiness, the just (right), which is decreed and must be heeded, making grace, salvation and order possible and demanding them at the same time. The knowledge which rules and rises in the covenant between God and Israel is compared to that in the perfect marriage covenant between man and wife: It is a knowledge made possible through the inclusive space of covenant and faithfulness, embracing and "tasting" (Ps 34:9) the whole bodily Thou, binding for the future and for the sake of fruitfulness. God as Spouse places the fruit, in the form of the promise, into the womb of the people, and it will one day be carried to term and delivered, and will bear the names "God-with-us" and "Messiah", "Son of God" and "Son of Man". That Israel does not recognize this fruit as the fulfillment of every promise of the covenant is her tragedy, which we do not need to deal with here, because God in his faithfulness even through all judgments does not retreat from the covenant he entered, and he will finally (Rom 11) make known the truth of his first choice. It is much more important that, just as in a child the portions from man and woman grow together into absolute indistinguishability, so in the fruit of the covenant, the Messiah, the portion from God (who always retains the initiative, because he is God) and the portion from man fuse into an indistinguishable unity. In the Old Testament the Word of God, feared, praised and longed for (Ps 119), even so remained always hovering over Israel's head; therefore Israel's most perfect response lay not in its existential obedience (this was lacking again and again), but in its "praises", which were an answer on the level of the human word to the word of God—an answer which the Holy Spirit found worthy of being incorporated into the inspired Word of God itself. In Jesus Christ, on the other hand, the Word has become flesh, both members of the covenant are represented by the same person, and God's *sedaka* (which the Septuagint must translate as *dikaiosyne*, since it lacks a better word) is perfectly fulfilled on both sides: The Word of God is wholly realized in man, and man is wholly obedient to God in love, faithfulness, patience and suffering. In the Old Testament the unfulfilled space always had to be crossed and held together somehow by a "mediator": descending with the ten commandments written by God's finger on stone, ascending laden with the sins of the people and interceding

with fasts, prostrate before God's countenance
(Dt 9:18, etc.); the image undergoes a series of
variations all the way to the "servant of God". In
the New Testament the concept "mediator" is
only to be used in a figurative sense (1 Tim 2:5, to
state its singularity), and seen more deeply it is
obsolete: "There can be no mediator when only
one person is involved; and God is one" (Gal
3:20), namely, on God's side as well as on man's,
the realized, unique *dikaiosyne Theou*. Jesus Christ
makes it less than ever possible even slightly to
divide theology and spirituality; his "knowledge"
of God (as especially John 3:11, among other
texts, describes it) is one with his devoted attitude
of service (true witness as not seeking his own
glory, Jn 7:18): "Yes, I know him well, and I keep
his word" (Jn 8:55); in Johannine terms it might as
well read: "I am his Word and keep his word." All
of Christ's followers, all "Christian faithful" are
placed into this fulfilled form of the covenant.
There is the eminent case of the "help-mate" of
the new Adam; in virtue of the grace of his cross,
she was allowed to speak the perfect Yes (as the
highest flower of Israel) to his Incarnation, and
this perfect Yes remains given as the exemplar to
the community of Christ, which began with her.
But there is also the case of all the remaining
"saints", who let themselves be expropriated into

Christ's personified "justice of God", to stand in the authority of Christ as his "ambassadors" in the "ministry of reconciliation" (2 Cor 5:18 f.). However differently formed their offices and charisms may be, none can dispense with the unity of theology and spirituality—of knowledge of God and acknowledging action—or destine the believer to be a specialist on one of the two sides.

In Paul's loose enumerations of charisms, which cannot be conclusively systematized, there are certainly several important gifts which concern themselves more strongly with the side of knowledge (that which later will be named "theology"). On the basis of Ephesians 4:11 one could distinguish Apostles, prophets and teachers as the leading groups, while the "evangelists" and "pastors" (elsewhere called "leaders", "overseers") may be considered the representatives of the Apostles in individual districts and communities. In this list, one might perceive a certain continuation of the Old Testament triad of "priests", "prophets" and "wise men" (Jer 18:18; cf. Ezek 7:56), or else, in terms of the matters they represent, that of Law, Prophecy and Wisdom—the three great articulations of the old covenant. In this light one could, in the list in Romans 12, assign the "leadership" and perhaps also the *diakonia* to the first, the "prophecy" to the second, and the

didaskalia and the *paraklesis* as well to the third
kind; in the somewhat differently structured list in
1 Corinthians 12:18 ff., prophecy and the gift of
tongues as well as their interpretation could be
assigned to the second, *sophia* and *gnosis* but also
"discernment of spirits" to the third. 1 Corinthians
12:28 begins the list again with a clear primary
division: "God has set up in the Church first
Apostles, second prophets, third teachers", and
only then do the species and subdivisions partially
follow, as in the other lists. As against these
three groups, and not to be reduced to them,
would stand the predominantly practical charisms
such as "giving alms", "hospitality", "practicing
charity", "miraculous healings" and so forth. But
one should be aware that we are here at the root of
a differentiation between "doctrine" and "praxis",
and in no way at the root of a differentiation
between "theology and spirituality". On the one
hand, the first three categories are not sharply set
off from one another: Paul as Apostle possesses
the prophetic gift of tongues (1 Cor 14:18) and can
characterize himself as *didaskalos* (1 Tim 2:7; 2 Tim
1:11), and the close connection between "pastors
and teachers" in Ephesians 4:12 shows that both
functions are usually carried out by one person:
The leader is also catechist. On the other hand, the
same radical self-surrender to God in following

Christ to the Cross is demanded of the Apostle,
and doubtless also of the prophet and the teacher,
which is demanded of the more practically active
members of the community. Otherwise they could
not proclaim God's "mysterious, hidden wisdom",
which the leaders of the world did not know, since
if they had they "would never have crucified the
Lord of glory" (1 Cor 2:6 ff.): the wisdom that
is identical with "Christ crucified—a stumbling
block to Jews, and an absurdity to Gentiles" (1
Cor 1:23 ff.), which remains hidden from the
clever and wise, while it is revealed to the simple
(Mt 11:25). This integrated simplicity leads back
again into the mystery of Christ, because it expresses the human correspondence to God's indivisible simplicity (*haplotes*, cf. Mt 6:22 and parallels,
2 Cor 11:3; Eph 6:5) as well as the childlikeness
and apparent immaturity (*nēpios*, Mt 11:25) of
the man obeying God (cf. 1 Cor 1:26 ff.: "absurd",
"weak", "lowborn and despised", "those who
count for nothing"). Precisely this tension in the
Pauline concept of Christian *sophia*—which can
only be the wisdom of the Cross—shows that
even in the "theological" charisms, not the slightest
separation is seen between theory and spirituality.

But the problem must still be considered as to
what form "theology" can acquire so that something like "spirituality" could join with it—either

as contrast or as complement. Our point of departure was the Old Testament covenant in which the gracious God and the elect and claimed man turn to each other in a closing circle. For the Israelites, absolutely all truth lies within this sphere; and what lies outside this sphere (for example, the relationship of other peoples to their gods) or at least transcends this sphere (the relationship of Israel to other peoples) must be unconditionally viewed and evaluated by the truth contained in the sphere. But since on a simply practical level such a relationship was set between Inside and Outside, and since at the same time the prohibition existed against interpreting the Outside otherwise than in terms of the Inside, speculation became necessary on how the Outside stood in relation to truth. That is to say: the inner circle has the tendency to expand, without damage to its form, in the direction of a universality of truth. The many ways in which this broadening occurred in Israel cannot be presented here; they are present above all in the third circle of Old Testament thought, in the "wisdom". God chose Israel freely, and that already shows that he is after all the Lord of all the nations (Dt 7:7). Therefore he is also Lord of the remaining gods (Ps 95:3; 96:4 and others), who thereby are reduced to his vassals, but as gods to "nothings". In Daniel they become angels of the nations, through whom the only true God rules the remaining peoples and their history. And though Zion is the place of his presence, yet the whole earth, indeed the cosmos, is irradiated by his glory and must praise him as Lord. So he becomes Lord of the most remote past—the creator of the world (Gen 1:1)—as well as Lord of the farthest future (Is 46:8 ff.). And this broadening must prove itself at some point; what now appears as a narrow circle of covenant will one day embrace everything. In this certainty the Priestly text can place the universal Noah-covenant before the covenant with Abraham as its anticipation. From within, then, and without abandoning its unique center, the finite expands itself to the infinite.

This prepared universality is realized in principle through God's becoming *man*. By virtue of his Resurrection the rabbi from Nazareth is exalted to be Kyrios over the entire creation, before whom all knees are to bend. But the faithful who are sent into the world must cooperate in carrying out this claim, which is grounded on a factual sovereignty (Mt 28:18–20; Acts 1:8). In principle, this must occur by their bearing the truth of the New Testament into the world through preaching and example. It need not be especially shown here by texts to what extent preaching and example must occur in complete unity (the model of Paul,

1 Peter, etc.). On the other hand, the sermon presents a three-fold problem: first, the whole of the internal truth of the covenant must be brought into the service of preaching in a form that can somehow be seen in its entirety; that is, since Christ through his existence established this form, it must now be reflected upon and clothed in words and concepts. Second, this kerygma must be presented—and consequently appropriately translated—in a conceptual language, so that it can be understood by those who stand outside. But for this—third—the standpoint of those outside must be known, along with the perspective which reaches from the outside to the proclaimed inner space. But this means that the person proclaiming must not only think from within to the outside, but must be able, in the service of his message, to accompany the listener step by step from outside into the interior. The first aspect, reflection on the entirety of God's revelation in his covenant with humanity, we will call "theology" in the special sense (ranging from God who speaks, down to human speech concerning this Word of God). The second is either "apologetics" or theology with apologetical pertinence, and the third would best be called "theological dialogics", because the preacher of Christ walks the path toward the center of Christian truth together with the

one who stands outside, in conversation with him, considering his objections and taking them seriously. A fourth aspect has not yet even been mentioned which played perhaps the greatest rôle in the unfolding of Christian theology: the demarcation necessitated by misinterpretations, false doctrines and schisms, and the resulting reflection on the genuine core of truth and its best possible expression in words.[1] Instead of "best possible" one really should say "authentic"; that would raise the whole problem between office and doctrine (theology), which concerns us only indirectly here. But it must at least be indicated: If Christ, the obedient servant of the Father and the one exalted to Kyrios, is the infallible truth of the covenant (that means the truth of God in the world, as well as the truth of mankind for God), where is the guarantee that this infallible truth is held without

[1] "Through the heretics the Catholic Church was expressed in words, and through the false thinkers the right-thinking people were preserved. . . . For example, had the Trinity been completely treated before the Arians blasphemed against it? Or had penance been completely treated before the Novatians resisted? Thus Baptism, too, was not fully treated before the expelled Anabaptists spoke against it, nor had that which was said about the unity of Christ been said in such a developed, explicit way; rather, it was first expressed thus when that division began to trouble the weak brethren. . .": Augustine, *En. in Ps.* 54, 22 (PL 36, 6430).

deviation by the Church and is rightly expressed in preaching? The guarantee lies first of all in the meditation of that Church, who is truly "without blemish and wrinkle" and who treasures all the words of God and Christ in her heart (Lk 2:20, 51) in order to perform them in faith (Lk 11:27 f.). But nothing in the Church of sinners can fully correspond to this inner, unique norm, except the guarantee given likewise to the Church as part of her constitution, the guarantee of maintaining the right course in things of faith and of action, and consequently, too, of giving the authentic directives in theological interpretation. This authority, however, lies in and beyond "prophecy" and theologically interpreting "wisdom". The decision-making authority comes into action precisely in the defense against heresy, and because these drawings of boundaries scarcely occur without severity, at times merciless severity, theology is in danger in this area of becoming theoretical and distancing itself from *praxis* (which, in Christian terms, is always love). Here above all we see, in the writings of the Fathers of the Church, a dualism that arises between a polemical theology which threatens to lose itself in conceptual subtleties (though they are unavoidable), and undisputed theology within the Church which develops out of the fullness of the covenant idea. What irony is present even in Irenaeus, to say nothing of the contentious tone of Tertullian and lesser writers! What a difference exists between certain trinitarian-polemical writings by Gregory of Nyssa and his "mystical" writings! We see the fracture lines even in the speeches of Gregory Nazianzen, where he tries to melt the two theologies into one another. In contrast, Origen gives a radiant counter-example which continues to be effective even after the condemnations, because he develops his universal theology out of the one center of Scripture, which he sees from the very beginning in its multi-dimensionality: in the literal (historical) and the spiritual sense, then in the tropological (action in this aeon) and the anagogical (toward the coming aeon) senses. These dimensions are not added belatedly to the sense of Scripture—as for example, in the modern era, the "practical corollaries" of a spiritual theology are brought to the theoretical truth of the "dogmatic"—they are, rather, the inner dimensions of the meaning of Scripture itself. Henri de Lubac[2] did not tire of showing that the first axis is identical, at the most profound level, with the transcendence from the Old to the New Testament, from the Law and

[2] *Histoire et esprit* (Paris: Aubier-Montaigne, 1950); *Exégèse médiévale*, 4 vols. (Paris: Aubier-Montaigne, 1959–1964); and numerous individual essays.

the prophets and wisdom to the gospel of Jesus Christ, who as such is the spiritual sense of all of Scripture. And this spiritual sense, which cannot lie only in a static understanding, releases out of itself, again, the dimensions of the second axis: Knowledge is realized in deed and at the same time in self-surmounting (following the crucified and risen Lord) to the aeon of the coming perfection. If this is the basic structure of Christian revelation, we stand once again beyond every possible separation between theoretical and spiritual theology; such a separation, in fact, exists nowhere in Origen's work. I have indicated elsewhere[3] that the four senses of Scripture are celebrating a hidden resurrection in the most modern Protestant theology, where the "literal sense" appears as the "historical-critical" sense, to be reached by research, the "spiritual" as the "kerygmatic", the "tropological" as the "existential", and the "anagogical" as the "eschatological". For Bultmann, moreover, as for Origen, the existential and eschatological senses are nothing but a nearer characterization of the kerygmatic sense. We will return to the difference between the two theologies.

[3] Introduction to de Lubac's work *Histoire et Esprit* in the German translation: *Geist aus der Geschichte* (Einsiedeln: Johannes Verlag, 1968).

The separation between the polemical-abstract theology after Origen, which led to conciliar definitions, and the inner-biblical theology was once more largely overcome in the West, though not fully, with Augustine. While, for example, the *Enarrationes in Psalmos* are almost wholly inner-biblical elaborations, the division runs through *De Trinitate*, as well as through the many polemical writings. Still, the abstract formulas remain very much filled by the life-blood of biblical contemplation. The fight against heresy is felt as a burdensome duty of the shepherd; in preaching the shepherd is already more free, but now and then he must make his little sheep aware of the threatening danger; in the contemplation of the Word (Genesis, the Psalms, John) and in the contemplation—perhaps too much emphasized! —of the self beneath the Word (*Confessiones*) he reaches his most proper concern. But thereby it is also clear that we are no longer confronted with Origen, who, with the impetus of a theology that was still young, had gathered in the entire knowledge of the world, from the innermost core (the covenant theology) outward in expanding circles. In this expansion he also encounters the "philosophy" of other cultures and religions; they are brought to their "truth" in the single Logos of God, who became man in Christ. And this progressive widening and inclusion of all truth in theology knew no break between the edifying homily to the people and the learned commentary; one cannot really contrast these two categories in Origen's work. Augustine introduces a new period, as becomes evident in the writings of Gregory the Great and his following: The labors of the pastor in the old aeon are hard and pressing, and the soul flees for refreshment into the "spiritual sense", which becomes the "mystical" (thus, more than "eschatological"). The turning from Origen to Evagrius, "Marcarius", Cassian—in short, to monasticism—stands behind this; and the dangerous separation threatens here in a new way.

But it is precisely the monasticism of the early Middle Ages which succeeds in almost wholly closing the gap—within the confines of the monastery, certainly, in a translation of Origen's synthesis into the dimensions and the needs of monastic existence. In his masterful book *L'Amour des lettres et le désir de Dieu*,[4] Jean Leclercq has described for us this unique synthesis, which extends from Gregory and Bede to the school of St. Victor and its contemporaries, and whose

[4] Paris: Editions du Cerf, 1957.

center and pinnacle are the works of Bernard. It is important that the breadth to the world is not lacking (the monks save the philosophy and literature of antiquity), and yet the steep summit of this theology lies in the Song of Songs as the central mystery of creation and covenant, of Church and soul, in which *eros* sublimates itself entirely in *caritas*. The unity seems to have been achieved once again without a seam, though essentially on the basis of monastic, contemplative existence; not without reason did Anselm perceive Roscelin—as Bernard perceived Abelard and Gerhoh the "novitates"—as a threat at the roots. The contemplatives themselves become harsh and polemical against a new way of thinking that is no longer bound to the monastery: Francis and Dominic press forth into the world, and their disciples must principally climb over the walls of the monastery; the university is a secular place, and worldly teachers and methods of thought take their place—in dialogue and polemics—beside spiritual ones. The discussion with Judaism and Islam creates something like an ecumenical situation (Thomas, Roger Bacon, Lullus, Cusanus). The tension mounts as the philosophical methods of thought (Aristotle) are pressed into the service of theological reflection and as theology is thereby conclusively made a "science";[5] it increases when Thomas is succeeded by the fall into nominalism, which for the first time allows an irreconcilable opposition to arise between (scholastic) theology and spirituality (*devotio moderna*, Erasmus). The Reformation will seek an escape from this opposition; and yet this tension becomes fruitful once more as the Franciscans and the Preaching Friars, each in a different way, attempt to master the whole arch of theology: Bonaventure, as he tries to include in his later syntheses the anti-scholastic spirituality of the Franciscans who follow Joachim of Fior; Eckhart, Seuse, Tauler (and also John of the Cross), who decisively fling wide the door to mysticism which was opened with Thomas. Nevertheless, the two pillars on which this arch rests have developed too far apart from each other for the arch to be safely placed. Thus, the neoscholasticism of the Counter-Reformation becomes the classic era of the separation between theoretical and affective theology: on the one hand a dry process of distinction, no longer borne and justified by the object, and on the other hand a spiritual theology which is no longer nourished by the center of revelation. We need waste no words

[5] Marie Dominique Chenu, *La Théologie au XIIe siècle* (Paris: J. Vrin, 1957); idem, *La Théologie comme science au XIIIe siècle*, 2nd ed. (Paris: J. Vrin, 1943) (pro manuscripto).

on the excesses of the theoretical theology of the baroque era: its weakness clearly lies in the fact that it is no longer a central meditation on the biblical revelation, but proceeds from a fixed "teaching of the Church" as object and therefore misses the spiritual, existential dimension which runs through everything biblical. It is stranger that the so-called affective theology of the baroque, which is objectively already what the nineteenth century will call "spirituality", also misses this biblical center and—increasing the onesidedness of the monk- and nun-theology of the early and late Middle Ages, which had already become one-sided—proceeds "mystically" instead of eschatologically, introvertedly instead of in a way that is open to the world, and above all anthropocentrically instead of truly soteriologically. This applies, upon closer examination, even to the greatest names such as Francis de Sales, Bérulle, and Fénelon, in whose writings—despite everything valuable for which we must still thank them today—the concern is essentially for the progress of the devout, pious self, the "Philothea". Henri Bremond was able to summarize the whole splendid and yet secretly tragic history of this era under the horrible, fundamentally Schleiermacherian title of *Histoire du sentiment religieux en France* (in Spain and Germany it would have been hard to find something different—only something less valuable). There are exceptions: Pascal goes beyond the boundary in his *Pensées* toward the synthesis which was indicated in Origen; Marie de l'Incarnation (as well, naturally, as Ignatius of Loyola) goes beyond the preoccupation with the pious self toward an apprehension of the gospel as a whole. But, oddly, a real attempt to bring to light the "theology of the Exercises"—beyond scholasticism and spirituality—was not made until the twentieth century.[6] So this work, the fundamental theological vision of the *Societas Jesu* (of those joined anew with Jesus) remained without the expected theological fruit: the re-insertion of theology as a whole into the core of the original encounter between God who calls and sends and the pardoned man who is sent in obedience. The opening of the *Societas* beyond its own organization to the entire Church, and through it to the world, could also have stimulated this opening of its theology together with spirituality; nevertheless, the return to re-actualizing the Bible in the

[6] Erich Przywara, *Deus semper maior: Theologie der Exerzitien*, 2nd ed., 2 vols. (Vienna: Herold, 1964); G. Fessard, *La Dialectique des exercices spirituels de S. Ignace de Loyola*, 2 vols. (Paris: Aubier-Montaigne, 1955 and 1966); Karl Rahner, *Betrachtungen zum ignatianischen Exerzitienbuch* (Munich: Kösel Verlag, 1965).

works of Ignatius did not have the profound effect which occurred with the Reformers.

The Reformation, with its return to Scripture, was a great attempt to overcome at its base the duality between scholastic and spiritual theology. The very complicated history of its turning-points cannot be traced here; everyone knows of its salutary effects on the modern Catholic biblical theology of the last decades, which was finally forced, by the earnestness as well as the radicality of the Protestant biblical inquiry, to take up the questions in its own way, and thus was able to assume, though with critical evaluation, much that stood ready. Attention should be called to one point:[7] that for Luther the actual "partner of God" was not the people (and thus the objective consciousness of the Church), but the self; and that the basic question for him was not: How do I correspond to God's call of grace (Ignatius asked this), but: "How do I get a gracious God?" This double shift in the heart of the subject-matter had a great effect throughout the centuries. On one hand the ecclesiastical norm and authority between the word of God and the existential, listening self was left out, and on the other hand

[7] On the following, cf. my essay "Zwei Glaubensweisen" in *Hochland* 59 (1967): 401–12; reprinted in *Spiritus Creator* (Einsiedeln: Johannes Verlag, 1967), 76–91.

the self did not turn its inquiry totally away from itself and to the Word of God, but applied this word as a longed-for remedy to its own dreadful situation. The Pauline *"pro me"* (Gal 2:20) was shifted in a way which at first glance seemed imperceptible (because the text in Galatians applies essentially to the faith-existence), but had devastating effects.[8] The issue is now the effect wrought in the self (perceptible in the self's reflection on the faith) by the Word which gives pardon; therefore (especially since the Kantian separation between theoretical and practical reason) what has historically occurred can be increasingly detached from what is existentially important. The stages go from pietism to Schleiermacher and to his radicalization in the "value" thought of Ritschl on the one hand and of W. Herrmann, who was the teacher of both K. Barth and R. Bultmann, on the other. From Herrmann to Bultmann the old separation of theology and spirituality arose in a wholly new and virulent form: "objective" theology, insofar as it is interested in the objective (or dogmatically objectivized) "facts of salvation", becomes frankly unimportant for the believer; only the existential

[8] On this point, see the fundamental book by Paul Hacker, *Das Ich im Glauben bei Martin Luther* (Graz: Styria, 1966).

connection between the spoken kerygma (in which the pardoning God with his disposition to salvation is present) and the self who is coming under the judgment of this word, has Christian significance. Theology dissolved into the "historical-critical method" on the one hand and into the spirituality of the connection between Word and existence on the other.

Although such a theology distances itself to such an extent from the true fundamental biblical substance, where the issue is never the solitary self but the We of people, community and Church, never the relating of the Word to oneself, but relating oneself to the Word ("no longer I live . . .")— nevertheless this much remains to be learned from it: The revelation of God in the Old and New Testaments is not primarily a doctrine but the occurrence of a deed, which must therefore be answered not with (faith-) knowledge, but with a life (in the Holy Spirit). In this regard Catholics must let Herrmann's intense anti-Catholic invectives take effect on them, and also the attacks —which have become really timely in the post-conciliar situation—of Karl Barth, who lumps together Catholicism and Schleiermacherism, that is, Protestant modernism. Only the person who has really listened here will be able to respond appropriately. There can certainly be no talk of our being able to separate the historical Jesus from the Christ of faith as irrelevant. Many of Bultmann's disciples are already on the way back from this construction, which liquidates Christianity; suddenly they are concerned again with the attitude of the historical Jesus (which G. Ebeling characterizes as "faith") and with the (Ignatian!) problem of following, which occupies for example E. Fuchs (as previously D. Bonhoeffer). Laboriously, the unity of theology and spirituality is being worked on anew, and this time under portents which are less directly threatened by the shadow of Luther. But the work is still just beginning.

An oft-stated fact: the young generation can scarcely be interested any more in Luther's basic question, "How do I get a gracious God?" It is not personal, isolated justification which interests them, but first of all the solidarity of mankind in need and in hope for salvation, and then the realization so urgently demanded by the gospel. While, with the first concern, they find their way back to an anti-individualistic understanding of community (and thus to something like Church, above all as a community occurring *in actu*), with the second they find their way back to a long neglected aspect of biblical spirituality, perhaps never so strongly seen as it is today. Christianity is not only to be received in faith, nor only preached, but performed. And not only through individuals, like Peter Claver or Las Casas or Vincent de Paul, nor only through a minority which is soon trampled down again (the Paraguay experiment), but through the involvement of the Church as a whole in the entire world. "Political theology", then, but no longer in the dimensions of the Constantinian era (which extends, inclusively, to the nationalism of modern times), where the sphere of "Church" coincides with the domain of "empire" and expands together with it (and by its methods of expansion); nor corresponding to the concept of the West and its tense political discussion between the "Christian nations", in any event with their expansions into the rest of the world as colonial territory; but where the sphere Church *must* fall together with the sphere World, and in this postulate the center of Christian existence (as mission) is seen: at the intersection, then, of Is and Ought. And this Ought would now be free from over-hasty identification with the earthly "empire" (and its instruments of power and methods of government), and placed instead on the means of the mere gospel, which are less, and at the same time infinitely more, than those methods. This turning should not be set aside too quickly with the catch-word Pelagianism; rather,

one should consider that the man Jesus was engaged
in physical labor for thirty years before he became
engaged in spiritual work for three years, to suffer
at last the *triduum mortis*. The suffering, though
it was the goal of his whole existence, was at the
same time the crowning conclusion of an effort to
realize the *polis* of God on earth; in *this* sense, Jesus'
life as a whole is political theology. A generation
which has a sense for this and which no longer
tolerates the separation between theology and
spirituality, contemplation and action, Church
and world, should not have its wings broken
at the outset. But it must learn to understand
that Christ's action commits him more profoundly
than anybody else; that God takes him more
seriously at his word; that the Passion, as a bearing
of the sin of the world and descent into the hell of
Godforsakenness, is the divine way of making
true in him that which he always wanted and
sought: that the Father's will be done on earth
as it is in heaven. Anyone who is not focused
from the very beginning on this total obedience
to the Father's ways with the Son should as a
Christian keep his hands off of political theology.
For it is from the last assent that all Christian
realization receives its meaning and its fruitfulness.
What is not built on this foundation—Paul is
speaking of the Cross and Resurrection of Christ—

remains wood, hay and straw (1 Cor 3:12). This presupposes, of course, what Paul also presupposes in those lines: that the Christ of faith is identical with the Jesus of history—how else could Paul set his existence on him who "offered himself up for me", and how could he bear "the marks of his wounds on my body"—and thus that all (political) spirituality grows out of an ecclesiastical faith (which must be "dogmatically" explained and understood) in Jesus Christ and in the implications of this faith: Trinity and Ecclesiology with all its components, the theological doctrine of creation, and eschatology.

We went out from the ring of the covenant: God reveals himself—and thereby his *essence*!—to man in deeds, which at the same time become understandable words; man answers this self-disclosure as the chosen one, the favored one, the one called, by attempting as a *whole* person (soul and body, prayer and action, inwardness and relation to the world) to form himself in his existence into an answer to God's call. Then he, too, is laid open and revealed in his *essence*. Thereby he becomes a "mirror" (2 Cor 3:18) of God in the world, as Jesus Christ was originally as the "image", "expression" and "reflection" of the Father. If this mirror were pure, one would have to see the whole prototype reflected in it. Thus Christian *praxis* or spirituality would have to mirror the whole Christian theory or dogmatics. The Pauline epistles can demonstrate that this is correct: from the practical sections the dogmatic section could be reconstructed in all essentials, should it ever be lost. From this perspective one may ask if it makes sense to continue distinguishing between theology and spirituality in the future. In Origen, as we saw, such a distinction was not made. The distinction is necessary as make-shift where dogmatics (above all through polemical controversy) has become so conceptualized that part of the succulence which characterizes the Word of God everywhere is lost. Yet history has demonstrated that the juice, served up in a special dish, cannot give the main dish back its flavor. Flesh and blood must be together originally in order to live; they cannot be brought together after the fact into something living. It has been shown elsewhere[9] that the history of theology proves this statement: Only those theologies became vitally effective in history which bore their spirituality not as an addition but within themselves, which embodied it in their innermost being. In conclusion we

[9] By the author, "Theologie und Heiligkeit" (1948) in *Verbum Caro, Skizzen aus Theologie* (Einsiedeln: Johannes Verlag, 1960), vol. 1, 195–225; and especially idem, *Herrlichkeit* vol. II: *Fächer der Stile* (Einsiedeln: Johannes Verlag, 1962).

can state that only such an integrated theology has a chance to enter convincingly into the ecumenical dialogue. The differences can in no case be thoroughly dealt with by means of various abstract dogmatics, for in their abstraction they are not "capable of resolution"; the differences can only be handled by living organisms which have a capacity to meet and understand each other, only because they all can be animated by just *one* life: that of God in Christ.

THE UNITY OF THE
THEOLOGICAL SCIENCES

1. The Scientific Structure of Theology

That "theology" is a science at all in a sense identical with other sciences, or even in an analogous sense, was by no means always certain. For the Fathers theology was the somehow conclusive *gnosis* that brought to truth that which the Greeks and other nations designated as "philosophy" (which always included a doctrine about divinity or the gods). In the early Middle Ages the existential aspect was emphasized: theology stands higher than (simply theoretical) science; it is wisdom, *sapientia* (from *sapere*: to taste, to experimentally savor); God gives himself in his self-revelation from outside (in salvation history) and inside (in infused faith, hope and love) to participation. In the transition to high scholasticism and with the precision of the concept of science brought about by the rising Aristotelianism, the problem became topical: Thomas presented a preliminarily conclusive solution which included many of the lines of thought pursued by his predecessors. Sciences are not simply autonomous, but always need to assume ("believe") certain statements or results from other sciences, together with which they deal with the whole field of reality, which is everywhere interconnected. Now there is a twofold science about God. One aspect proceeds from the evidence of the human principles of reason, which are bound to the senses, in order to think toward the origin of things: philosophy (or "natural theology"). The other acts "according to the way of the Divine itself, so that this will be grasped in itself; for us on earth this is only imperfectly possible; nevertheless, there is a participation in and assimilation to the self-knowledge of God, when we, through the faith given us, cling to (acknowledge the rightness of) the original truth for its own sake."[1] Thomas therefore asserts an analogy (not an identity) between the structure of natural reason (what is given by the senses and is worked upon by the light of pure reason, which corresponds to the basic disposition for "being as a whole") and the structure of theological reason (what is historically given—the Bible, summarized in the

[1] *In Boeth. De Trin.*, q 2 a 2c.

Creed and kerygma, believed and worked upon with progressive understanding through the light of faith, which is a certain participation in God's self-contemplation and in the vision of God which the blessed have).[2] Because human reason is required in the second case as well, to penetrate with its own powers of thought (supported by grace) what is put before it to be believed, because it is required to see connections and deduce consequences, theological work truly receives a genuinely scientific character.

Two things about this conception, which is still worthy of attention today, seem strange to us. The first is the fixation of the object to the *sacra pagina*, the Holy Scripture (this formulation is sanctioned by patristic tradition and will be radicalized once more in the Reformation) or even to its summary in the "Articuli" of the Confession of Faith. To these were added secondarily their interpretations through Tradition as "*Sententiae*",[3] and finally the rational inquiries (*Questionaes*) by the Magistri; and these latter represented the present state of the science, so to speak. Today, in the historical era, we would designate the actual object not as something standing *behind* Scripture,

[2] In *1 Sent* prol a 5; *In Boeth. De Trin.* q 3 a 4 ad 4.

[3] First comprehensively codified by Peter Lombard, the "Master of Sentences".

but certainly as something attested to and aimed at by Scripture: the living history of God with man whom he has chosen as partner. With this, the second oddity would vanish as well; because then faith does not refer, for us, to the letter of Scripture, or to the Articles of Faith, or to dogmatic formulations, but rather—as in the occurrence of the Old and New Testaments—solely to the living God, who reveals himself nowhere in a naked as-such (if that were even thinkable), but in the deeds, guidances and assistances which proclaim him, in his directions and commandments, his promises and fulfillments for man, all of them events which—as is appropriate to the deepest essence of encounter—enter again and again into words and finally into a Word-form which— answered for by God's Spirit—attests to his history with man, and, through the same Spirit, makes it for all the future ever newly present and an event.

Without the concept of analogy, the inquiry into the scientific structure of theology will fail. For theology cannot possibly be counted univocally among the other sciences (which argue from the highest principles evident to reason); belief in "that which is presented for belief" (whether in statements or in historical events) remains its basis and prerequisite. On the other hand, it can only be called a science (analogously) when what is received in faith can be assimilated and understood in a genuine effort of reason. This indicates two things. First, it belongs to the essence of this and *only* this science that its scientific objectivity rests on the decision to believe, and that there can be, therefore (theologically considered), no neutral objectivity, no consideration of the object of belief without belief, or apart from belief and unbelief. The theory which was favored at the beginning of our century—in which objective scientific method and subjective commitment were regarded as separable—even should it be applicable elsewhere, cannot be used here. Second, the apparently total isolation of theology from the remaining sciences decreases when the sciences of the humanities (only in recent times really recognized in their essence) are seen and acknowledged as the inner-worldly proof of the analogy of sciences. There is also real science of the (relatively or wholly) unique, even when this unique object is only to be circled round and expressed with the instruments of various analogies. An historical event as well as a great, "unique" work of art can be an object of scientific research, and thereby of progressive knowledge as well—without the object ever being really "worked out", because the character of uniqueness (and, to that extent, incomparability) belongs to its essence. No computer will be able to deal conclusively with *The Magic Flute*; but perhaps it is precisely the "uniqueness" of a "congenial" interpreter which can most nearly approach the "wholly other" uniqueness of the magical work; and I myself in my uniqueness, through the mediation of a great teacher (learning to see through his eyes), glimpse the uniqueness of the work of art. If the analogy of the humanities is lacking, a "dialogue" between the natural sciences and theology might well be senseless and impossible; the humanly unique forms a bridge to the understanding of what is unique in the Bible, in Christianity.

Here is another approach. It is not to no purpose that the verb "to know" is used biblically in a strong sense of sexual union. "The man knew Eve his wife" (Gen 4:1). Let us understand this union in the comprehensive sense which lies within it objectively: mutual, complete devotion based on a spiritual life-bond, a final covenant and belonging-together; devotion which now transcends the separation of bodies and includes a boundless promise for the future. Such knowing is "unique" each time, because it actualizes the whole person intensively and extensively, and grants an insight (inner-sight) into the partner which can be gained in no other way. Now it is thoroughly possible that, for intellectually unspoiled, undistracted people, the meaning of their life, of their tribe, of the world around them and of life as a whole is ordered concentrically around the wisdom contained in this experience. And thus it is no accident but a supporting analogy when, in one of the greatest breakthroughs in understanding in the Bible—in Hosea—the relationship of man and wife becomes a sign of the relationship between Yahweh and Israel.[4] When we see in Yahweh the self-revealing

[4] H. W. Wolff, "Wissen um Gott bei Hosea als Urform von Theologie", in *Evangelische Theologie* 1952/53, 533 ff.; also in *Gesammelte Studien zum Alten Testament*, Theologische Bücherei 22 (Munich: C. Kaiser, 1964), 182–205, which, however, emphasizes the objective deeds of salvation and the corresponding rights of God, more than the traditional exegesis cited here. The issue is not "psychologizing interpretations", "familiar intercourse", "intimate contact" and similar things (199), but the unique, definitive truth produced in the uniqueness of the intercourse of man and wife. In the self-giving between man and wife there lies a mystery which is given naturally through the exclusivity and the total commitment in their encounter. Thus, too, only Israel in its devotion to God knows the mystery of his revelation. Pascal's dictum belongs here: "*Le coeur a ses raisons que le raison ne connaît pas.*" That is an echo of the medieval definitions of theology: Theology "has its own grounds and principles as against the other sciences, which, through the grace of faith,

one and the living God, in Israel the nation chosen by him in incomprehensible choice of love, and their turning to each other as "covenant", which can be violated and broken by man but which can be described as final for God (because of his absolute truth, fidelity and trustworthiness), then we have the original form of the object of theology, which will expand in various ways but will never change its basic composition. In anticipation of the second section we can say that the turning toward each other of God's self-revelation (as fidelity to created man and devotion to him) and the man pliant to (believing in) God has its meaning in the self-purposefulness of mutual love; the New Testament (as the fulfillment of the Old), without abolishing the "conjugal" exclusivity of this turning toward each other, will extend it to God's covenant with humanity in general, and will teach the interpretation of all of creation in this latter light. In this, the concreteness of the form (in Christ and the Church) will on the one hand remain; on the other hand, the worldly systems, with the sciences belonging to them, appear included, certainly, but not called into question.

---

are evident and manifest to the soul illumined by faith, although they remain hidden to the unbelievers": E. Rigaud, *Quaestiones*, ed. Pergamo, in *Arch. franc. hist.* (1936), q. 1, 24 f.

The covenant is dialectical. Regarding the initiative, it can only be one-sided; there is no parley between God and man. This is shown by the establishment of the covenant in the call of Abraham and the great promise to him. But the covenant must also be two-sided, or else it is not a covenant. It must put man (by grace!) under obligation; this is shown by the sealing of the covenant with the people on Sinai. A law is necessarily added to the promise. The more the law—spoken by God's voice (Dt 5:22), written by his finger (Ex 34:1)—proves itself divine, the more man understands that he cannot keep it, and the more he needs, not only ritual atonement, but a human mediator who holds the breaking pieces together, who, atoning, represents God before the people and the people before God: like Moses (especially in Deuteronomy), the great prophets, and finally the "Servant of God". But the relationship will not be really healed until the covenant is fulfilled, "kept", concretized by God himself, until God's Word coincides with the obedient man, who as such not only (legally) represents the people, but, because he bears the guilt of all upon himself, has the people really within him: "head" of the "body", "living bread", which unites the many into "one body" (1 Cor 10:17). He is "made sin" personified (2 Cor 5:21) and can in the same act

become the personified "justice of God" for everyone (ibid.), because he alone embodies the covenant as God promised it and carried it out: Jesus
Christ, God and man. This fulfillment through
God does not indicate any overpowering of man's
freedom. As the Israelite was free to turn to God
and to turn away from him, so man remains free
when confronted with Christ to acknowledge his
claim or not. And if he acknowledges him and
comes under the statute of the fulfillment of the
convenant (and thus of eternal love's accomplishment, and therefore also the unity of love of God
and love of neighbor), he becomes truly free for
love for the first time. He stands under no compul-
sion of law, but receives, through the liberation of
Christ (Gal 5:1), the spirit of freedom (2 Cor 3:17),
the "law of perfect freedom" (James 2:12). In this
God not only sealed his work of creation, but in
his free creation and without infringing on its
freedom, reveals himself as he who he is; so much
so that with compelling logic he shows himself to
be he who *in himself* is love, or in other words
triune life. If the form of the old covenant were the
last word, we would never have been free of the
suspicion that God needs mankind in order to
have a partner for his love; we would have seen
through God in his weakness, would have exalted
gnosis over *agape* or (which is the same in modern

terms) invented an evolutionary system in which God perfects himself through creation as that which he is: triune love. The "great logic" (of Hegel) would have the last word, at which point atheism is already directly in sight.

But if God in himself is "that beyond which something greater cannot be thought" (Anselm), and if in his self-revelation to man, loving and saving him, he has let precisely this Greatest (better: the Ever-Greater which is never finally comprehensible to thought) shine out—which leaves him free, because he does not need man in order to love, and sets man free, because he can never be freer than when the absolute Spirit of divine freedom blows through him—then the form in which this happens and can be "seen" as having happened receives the character of a self-evident truth. To see it certainly requires "the eyes of faith".[5] But this form,[6] and not,

[5] As P. Rousselot says, with the patristic tradition (*Die Augen des Glaubens* [Einsiedeln: Johannes Verlag, 1963]); cf. Eph 1:18. "*Omnino habet oculos fides, et potentiores, et fortiores*": Augustine, *En. in Ps.* 145 n. 19 (PL 37, 1897). Thomas, *Summa Theologica* III, q 55 a 2 ad 1: "*oculata fides*".

[6] Without this concept one cannot grasp the center of theology; cf. my book *Schau der Gestalt* (= *Herrlichkeit* vol. I, 2nd ed. [Einsiedeln: Johannes Verlag, 1968] English ed.: *Glory of the Lord*, vol. 1: *Seeing the Form* [Edinburgh and San Francisco: T. & T. Clark and Ignatius Press, 1983]); also G.

as the scholastics thought,[7] the *"articuli fidei"* taken individually, possesses the "self-evidence" (as W. Pannenburg also correctly says[8]). Nor is it so self-enclosed that God would not give human reason sufficient "signs" as open approaches, to enter on its own responsibility into the form. Abraham receives the "sign" of the wonderful birth of the son of the promise; Moses receives assurances for his mission; and the people continually receive confirmations that their decision to follow this God was, and remains, right. In

Koch, *Die Auferstehung Jesu Christi*, 2nd ed. (Tübingen: J. C. B. Mohr [P. Siebeck], 1965). I concur with Koch that the theological form is event (and thus cannot be disposed over) and that it occurs in the encounter, in the meeting of God and man in Christ.

[7] "In theology the first principles are the articles of faith, which, for those who have faith, are self-evident through the infused light": Thomas, *1 Sent.* prol. a 3, sol 2, ad 3.

[8] "The events in which God demonstrated his divinity are as such self-evident within their historical context. . . . The word of the kerygma is not itself the actual occurrence of revelation, but is an aspect of the revelation's occurrence, because it reports the eschatological event which in itself is a sufficient self-demonstration of God": Wolfhart Pannenburg, "Dogmatische Thesen zur Lehre von der Offenbarung", in *Offenbarung als Geschichte*, ed. Wolfhart Pannenburg, 2nd ed. (Göttingen: Vandenhoeck und Ruprecht, 1963), 113 ff. For the Catholic, of course, this self-evidence of God remains one of faith; see footnote 5, above.

spite of this, the absolute risk of self-giving must stand at the center as the only appropriate response to the "groundless" election of precisely *this* people (Dt 7:7; 8:17); this groundlessness of the love which is grounded only in itself, independent of all motivating characteristics of the beloved, was the striking comparison for the central theological event even for William of Auxerre.[9]

One more thing is essential. The subject which is taken into the covenant is centrally a people in the Old Testament (an individual only as a speaker to the people, or of the people to God). When the Word becomes flesh, it sums up in its "hiddenness" "all the treasures of the wisdom and knowledge of God", but they become "evident" only through the new people, the "Church" (Eph 3:10), who is to grow in totality and community into the overflowing fullness (Eph 3:18) and journey as a bride toward the eschatological "husband" (Eph 4:13). Thus the understanding of faith ("the understanding of the love of Christ which lies beyond all understanding": Eph 3:20) is an obligation, finally, of the Church: as her inner meditation through the millennia, insofar as she "is the maiden without wrinkle or blemish"

---

[9] William of Auxerre, *Summa Aurea*, ed. Philip Pigouchet (Paris: Nicolai Vaultier and Durandi Gerlier, 1500), Prologue, fol 2 ra; cf. ibid., lib. III, tr 3 c 1 q 1, fol 131 vb.

(cf. Lk 2:19, 51), and also as her definition (which literally means limiting) indicating direction, insofar as she, as the wandering people of God in history, needs an authority which leads with official competence. The short formulas of the Credo, the simplifications of the catechesis, and the formalized character of conciliar definitions will not be seen as exhaustive and certainly not as vessels replacing the content which always overflows them, but as indispensable emergency aids to order the fullness and to copy in sketchy fashion the unique, inimitable "form".

2. The Three Faces of Theology

The initially narrow form Yahweh-Israel, which is to transcend itself eschatologically even in the promises of the Old Testament, expands in Christ in such a way that he, to whom "all power is given in heaven and on earth", sends his messengers "to the ends of the earth", and accompanies their mission "until the end of the world". What was indicated dimly in the covenant with Noah—that God wills to make his covenant with all creation—fulfills itself bodily since the death and Resurrection of Christ, which proclaims God's reconciliation with the entire world (2 Cor 5:19;

Col 1:19 f.). But we have said that the universality of Christianity, the form placed into history (finally as Christ's death and Resurrection, in which the destiny of the world changes decisively), remains the indissoluble center, which as such rules throughout the earth and the universe as "head", but does not dissolve into them. This structure releases from itself, one after another, three distinct but inseparably connected theologies.

1. First there is the meditation on the form [*Gestalt*] of revelation, in order through understanding, insight and *sapientia* to attain more profoundly and correctly to realization (*fides quaerens intellectum*). This theology is predominantly contemplative, though not exclusively so, and it flourished from Augustine through Anselm and into the twelfth century: It consists in immersing oneself in individual events of salvation in order to fathom their divine dimensions, comparing situations or words in order to arrive at new perspectives (the "*spiritualia spiritualibus comparantes*" [1 Cor 2:14] of Origen). It is a way of thinking which is directed above all towards God, to praise and glorify the greatness of his gracious self-revelation. This form of theology is indispensable for all subsequent forms; it attempts to correspond responsively to the original encounter, God–Man. Its danger would lie in its isolating itself from the

others as the only form or the highest one: the danger of a merely contemplative foretasting of the eternal beatific vision of God.[10] However, God is to be given first honor in theology as well as everywhere else: not only with the lips or with the heart, but with the understanding, which, for love of God, attempts in respectful gratitude to understand what he has given us. From this *intellectus* the theology of the monks never separated *praxis*: existence as "praise of the glory of his grace" (Eph 1:6, 12:14). The whole person should, and desires to, respond to the gift which God the Father has made us in his Son by following him. Therefore the practical (paranetic) sections of the Pauline letters are so permeated with dogmatics that from them alone, if the theoretical sections were lost, his theology could be reconstructed. Therefore John simply equates *praxis* and the understanding of that which God

[10] The central explanation of the essence of theological science in Thomas Aquinas, through the "*subalternatio*" of the knowledge of faith (*lumen fidei*) under the divine and heavenly vision of truth, is influenced by this. Precisely the scientific endeavor is a dynamic toward the "vision": "*Tout ce travail, dans et sous la foi, tend à la vision*": Marie Dominique Chenu, *La Théologie comme science au XIIIe siècle*, 2nd ed. (Paris: J. Vrin, 1943) (pro manuscripto). Cf. Jean Leclerq, *L'Amour des lettres et le désir de Dieu: Initiation aux auteurs monastiques du moyen age* (Paris: J. Vrin, 1957).

is: Love (God) is known only by him who, in imitation of God, gives his life for his brothers. But with this the first circle, externally, is already opened to the second: Theology reflects on and regulates the kerygma of the messengers and witnesses of the faith who have been sent into all the world, to all the nations.

2. The theology oriented toward proclamation presupposes at its depths the universal validity of the particular historical acts of God in Jesus Christ (with his pre-history). The space in which this action takes effect, and which it originally means, is co-extensive with creation as a whole. The Holy Spirit effects this inner universalization (resurrected and exalted to *Kyrios*, Christ is already the "Spirit-Man") and consistently guides the transpositions of salvation history's expression in words, repeatedly necessary for this universal proclamation, into the kerygmatic forms and dimensions; the Hellenization of the Bible which had already taken place (the Septuagint) had performed decisive preliminary work in this direction. The demand for translation which lies in the command to be understandable to all nations is not free to make concessions ("teach them to observe *everything*"); the translation, then, must proceed ever anew out of the vision of the whole (the "first" theology), and is to make use of the

peoples' form of thought, in critical observation.
The Spirit-inspired, definitive word of witness
concerning God's act of salvation remains norma-
tive for proclamation, yet contains, not naked
facts, but a presentation of the facts which is
already "theologically" meditated in the people of
God—the two are inseparable. It is for this reason
that inner-biblical theology can never be elimina-
ted or simply relativized by a kerygma of a later
time, but must be included in the work of translation without suffering damage. Something analogous applies to directives decreed by ecclesiastical
authority for the interpretation of the basic articulations of the faith. The legacy of history and of
the spiritual work of God's people which is to
be included and considered does not signify any
limitation for today's messenger of the faith, but
is his guarantee that throughout this history he
stands in real contact with the central event of
salvation. Kerygma never accomplished something truly creative for a new time without the
transforming inclusion of the theology invested
in Scripture and tradition, even when it had to
establish new forms of expression in a fierce
struggle against what had been handed down
without reflection.

3. But in this second form the third is already
hidden. When he addresses his fellow man, the

person proclaiming the gospel cannot speak simply out of a general consideration of his environment; he must truly include his fellow man, drawing his foreign, unadapted standpoint into the event of the proclamation of the faith. This is realized very imperfectly by a so-called "apologetic theology", although it also has its justification: The apologist presents the form of revelation to the outsider in a manner which makes it appear plausible, coherent and acceptable to him from where he stands. But the apologist is engaged essentially in one-sided speech, or at best in the anticipatory refutation of possible objections. But according to the assumptions of the universality of the Christian salvation event which he defends, every other person is basically overtaken and taken in by Christ's grace (or at least by its offer). Each person, whoever he may be, is someone for whom God let his Son "be made sin" and let him die in Godforsakenness. Therefore his being loved by God and his capacity to correspond to the "unknown God" is to be given more credit than the apologist usually gives it. A "dialogical theology" is necessary here, in which the messenger of the faith takes his partner seriously as a brother in Christ in such a way that the two encounter each other under their mutual Lord and Judge. The Christian, therefore, will have to let his conversation partner speak to him about whatever appears inauthentic in himself or in the Church in whose name he speaks (for example, the divisions between the churches). In this dialogue he must humanly and personally make himself vulnerable—in such a way, certainly, that he neither relativizes nor risks the truth of his Lord. But he will recall that the salvation event which he proclaims deals with God's act of becoming completely vulnerable—even unto the opposite of himself, the worldliest world, Godforsakenness, malicious misunderstanding, betrayal, and so forth—in order to overtake the resisting opponent, man, through love, and in order to open him from within (by taking over his guilt). Dialogical theology, as opposed to kerygmatic, is no longer a theology which thinks from inside to outside, but rather one which leads step by step, in conversation with the brother, from outside to inside: a theology in the form of a *theologia crucis*, not merely by virtue of an inner (formal-logical) paradox, but of an existential realization, especially in the Christian, who can open to the Lord the other person's final otherness in being and thinking, no longer through words and arguments, but through . . . through what, indeed? perhaps through a silent, accompanying witness. Naturally we do not wish to establish a new theology by proposing this third form; rather, the so-called "apologetics" is to be shown its correct, complete form. Nor do we wish to advocate an equal status for all religions or false religions, for the Christian has perceived that in Christ God has acted not only uniquely ("once for all") but also unsurpassably (*"id, quo majus cogitari nequit"*). Yet the Christian must remain aware, not only that "there is something true" also in other points of view, but that the Christian truth is always greater than what he, in thinking, proclaiming, and indeed living, can capture; that he himself, then, precisely because he knows this, remains under the judgment of the Word he proclaims, and that this judgment can also meet him through his brother. Still less will he forget, next to the second form of the theology, the first form: the ever new immersion, in prayer and adoration, directly in the first truth, before striving for any kerygmatic and dialogical goals, in order to draw new power for proclamation and encounter by meditating on God's incomprehensible mystery of love. Thus the three forms of theology form a system of circulation. Or rather, it is the same face in three-fold, changing expression.

3. The Sciences of Theology

It is because theology possesses not only a material object (for example, the "articles of faith", which everyone perceives, and the collection of writings of the *biblia*, "books") but also an attitude of man—faith—which is inwardly implied in the object (in the salvation event in Christ) that the individual theological disciplines are held together through this inseparable material and formal aspect; even in increasing differentiation they remain dependent upon each other and mutually presuppose each other.

To begin in the innermost circle: It is clear that theoretical ("dogmatic") and practical ("ethical", "existential", "spiritual") theology can only work appropriately and develop prosperously in closest mutual action on each other. A dogmatics which degenerates into a pettifoggery far removed from life, a moral theology which degenerates into a casuistry far removed from the gospel, shift from the center to the perimeter and distort themselves. The object itself—the history of salvation in the Old and New Testaments, and its mirror, Scripture—shows the perpetual interrelation, on all levels and in all respects, of dogma and morals.

The concept of faith itself shows this *in nuce*: Faith is a surrender by man to the fidelity of God in which he agrees with God from the very beginning (it is faith *in* God's word) and adapts himself to that agreement (as trusting obedience of life).

Next we consider exegesis and dogmatics. In the beginning we showed that it is part of the scientific structure of theology that the decision between belief and disbelief in its object occurs ever anew. "Whoever is not for me is against me." Correspondingly, the Scriptures—when they are allowed to say what they want to say (and that is the first fundamental principle for every scientific philology)—are only interpreted objectively in their inclination toward their end (Christ and the Church), and whoever wants to interpret them differently, against this desired expression, must interpret them in the light of the general level of the religious phenomenon in the human race (thus "religious-historically"—"anthropologically"). In this, naturally, the religious-historical relationships (analogies or influences) can also be explored and freely determined when faith has been opted for; God's partner is, after all, the human being in his historical, cultural situation, which is connected with the rest of humanity. But the fundamental option of the researcher must reveal itself, in the long run, in the way in which the common ground (for example, that of Israel with the Near East) is classified and evaluated. The relative independence of the exegete does not, then, exempt him from the "ecclesiastical sense" (*sentire cum ecclesia*), to which his object itself finally directs him, even though he must remain in fruitful dialogue—which can often be an argument—with the dogmatic theologian. Further, he can work out and differentiate the individual "theologies" present in Scripture (theology of the deuteronomical historical works, of Paul, of Matthew, etc.). But in doing this he must not forget the extent to which these several and even contrary aspects grow out of a unity and return into it: It is the same old or new Israel which puts them forth from itself as legitimate forms of expression and takes them back in.[11] The contrasting of various biblical theologies, a method that is favored today, turns in the end to the greater honor of the God who in his revelation could afford such a multiplicity in unity.

Not only the exegete, but also the kerygmatic theologian (as preacher, catechist, teacher) and the dialogic theologian (the Christian in the world among unbelievers), because of the universal

[11] Cf. the following essay.

Christian sending into the world, will continually be in contact with non-theological sciences, whether these are carried on by Christians or non-Christians. Ecclesiology must accept the fact that its object is also handled by sociologists; catechists will be in contact with psychologists and demographers, and learn from them; the preacher and pastor will remain open to all forms of anthropology (to which medicine and psychiatry also belong). Christians do not thereby fundamentally step outside their domain, even though theology naturally cannot and should not absorb all these worldly sciences into itself. But the object of theology is so open that it must consider man, redeemed and claimed by God, in all his human relations, activities and destinies; it may not, for example, take him simply as an "immortal soul", for whose salvation in the beyond only the pastor and theologian should have to care. Yet this openness of theology to everything human should in no way tempt it to dissolve formlessly into the generally human; it retains its precisely definable focal point in God's historical salvific action, which has received such an infinite fullness in Christ, the "heir of all things" (Heb 1:2), that it cannot be surpassed by any human, world-historical evolution (which will never develop anything but the possibilities of *man*). This is indicated by the expression: God's action in Christ is eschatological; and all past and future history can only move toward this *eschaton* (Omega), whose full "theological" meaning will then reveal itself.

Openness and limit are equally granted to and fixed for the Christian theologian in his relationship to other religions and (in some circumstances atheistic) world views. Openness is granted and fixed insofar as he cannot prescribe for the universal grace of God in Christ which hidden ways it may make use of in order to allow as many men as possible—all men, if possible—to share in the final redemption. On the other hand, he has his defined, theological-kerygmatic commission; he is no "free scholar", but one sent, who is to work within the boundaries set for him. In the last Gospel Peter receives from the risen Lord the mission to feed his sheep and his lambs; he had to assert the "greater love" (which he had to borrow, so to speak, from the beloved disciple—but then, the two together form the one Church); but now he wants to know what will become of this beloved disciple, whom he still sees standing beside him. Christ's closing word to the visible Church as well as to the theologian ends with a reservation and a lordly question: "If I desire that he should remain until my return, what is that to you? You follow me!" (Jn 21:22). Thus the form of theology must, in the end—as long as it is *theologia viatorum*—remain unconcluded, because only the *Kyrios* has the full vision of the final form of revelation which his covenant with humanity possesses eschatologically.

THE MULTITUDE OF
BIBLICAL THEOLOGIES AND THE
SPIRIT OF UNITY IN THE CHURCH

1. Introduction

The situation of Christians today is confusing
and contradictory in many respects. There is the
contradiction within Catholicism that we wish to
go back behind all tradition and hear exclusively
the Word of God in the Bible, which, however,
tells us precisely what we do not want to hear
at any price—the eschatological message, the
alienation of Christians in the world, its hate and
persecution—where we would like to hear words
of "openness to the world" and of the earthly
future. This contradiction within Catholicism
will not be discussed here. But there is another
perplexing situation which is of considerable
ecumenical significance and which should occupy
us here: We seek to heal the split in the Church
by going back together from our dogmatics and
denominations to the *one* Word of God, and when

75

we hold the same Bible in our hands—soon, one hopes, a complete ecumenical Bible!—we discover that it no longer seems to offer, particularly today, the unity we wish to win from it because it has been split internally into a multitude of biblical theologies through modern exegesis. Certainly people have long spoken of Petrinism and Paulinism, of a Jacobine or a Johannine theology, and have built whole ecumenical syntheses on these (Schelling). But the task of binding into one single ecclesial theology such a plenitude of dissimilarities as the research on the Old and New Testaments has discovered and brought to light seems to go beyond the power of the individual churches and to cripple the enthusiasm in the ecumenical movement. In the moment in which we hold the Bible in our hands to seek the unity of the Church in it, the Bible itself seems to fail by falling apart into a multitude of theologies.

Nevertheless, let us not permit ourselves to be discouraged by this appearance. To use an illustration, it could be with this appearance as with a kaleidoscope: By a light shake of the instrument, ever new constellations, always complete and harmonious, come into being before the astonished eye; the "truth" is, on the one hand, that the same elements integrate themselves repeatedly into a new picture, and, on the other

hand, that where there is actually only one seg-
ment the appearance of a rounded whole is produced by the built-in mirrors. This illustration fits
insofar as in the Bible, too—out of its store of
perspectives—the same basic statements prevail
again and again, and insofar as there exist indissoluble cross-ties among all biblical theologies.
The illustration limps insofar as there also surface
in the Bible, not just apparent, but real figures,
finished "forms" [*Gestalten*], corresponding
to the internal and external impulse of every
human author to create forms.

As open as the problem presently remains,
let us not overlook at the beginning what a
great *enrichment* in understanding of Scripture the
modern research has brought us; where only
a two-dimensional plane seemed to be at hand
before, research has opened to us at least one
other, third, dimension. The texts become living
in an entirely new manner through the historical
limitations and variations appearing in them.
They begin to speak in a way in which they
could never speak earlier, and they carry on a
conversation among themselves which is at least
comparable to the ecumenical dialogue.

Nor, at the beginning, do we want to conceal
the problem of this new speaking of the texts.
Every science, in order to be a science, needs

a formal viewpoint and point of unity to which
the multitude of phenomena can be related and
from which they can be ordered and understood.
Bible science too, through which this new mani-
fold speech of the texts is released, needs such
a point in order to be science. Given that the New
Testament—and then Judaism, indeed the whole
Old Testament—revealed itself in this speech as
"an entirely . . . syncretic phenomenon",[1] then in
the face of such a determination there would be
only two possibilities. The first would be to let
the various conceptual languages of the Bible all
converge beyond themselves in that divine Lord
who turned to Israel in sovereign, free love,
and brought his promises to fulfillment in Jesus
Christ; and then all biblical theologies, as far as
they are clothed in human images and concepts,
would have to gaze, like the theologies of the
Church, up to this free Lord. If this possibility is
not accepted, there remains only the alternative of
seeking this point of unity which grounds Bible
science in the historical man and his understanding of himself—his pious or impious, theistic or

[1] H. Koester, "Häretiker im Urchristentum als theologisches
Problem", in *Zeit und Geschichte: Dankesgabe an R. Bultmann
zum 80. Geburtstag*, ed. E. Dinkler (Tübingen: Mohr, 1964),
64 f.

atheistic disposition. Certainly[2] both quantities—God and man—are continually encountered in the Bible, but there is no neutral ellipse around them. In the final instance there is only the either-or: Is God giving his view of man here, or man his view of God? Is biblical theology primarily the *Theos legon* or the *Theos legomenos*? But this question makes it clear that there is no such thing at all as neutral exegesis; rather, all exegesis, particularly if it wishes to be *scientific*, is faced with the fundamental decision of belief or unbelief, and accordingly the metal shavings of the texts arrange themselves around the magnetic center of God or of man. In the decisive questions (and these play into even the apparently most unimportant matters) there is no elimination of the "subjective value standards" from a "neutral, scientific" sphere; rather, the scientific character of the exegesis is precisely what demands the prior decision in light of which the interpretation is to take place. That is part of the uniqueness of theology's structure in the area of the sciences,[3] even though the remaining

[2] To the following, see above 17 ff., 55 ff.

[3] This unique structure, as is well known, caused the Middle Ages to hesitate over whether theology should be ranked among the sciences or should rather be characterized as the wisdom which elevates and concludes all sciences. Cf.

sciences, especially the humanities, do not lack
certain analogies (inner-worldly or under the influence of theology).[4] When the Bible is allowed
to say what it *wants* to say, and what it is capable
of saying with all clarity—indeed, it speaks of
nothing else—then it must be allowed to be God's
word to man. With this statement we have chosen
the standpoint of faith as the only one which does
justice to the phenomenon of the Bible. Assuming
this standpoint, we must further say that this
Word of God has certainly at first spoken "often
and in many forms" (Heb 1:1), but in order to sum
up all words in Christ into one single word which
contains all others within it, according to God's
plan of the history of salvation.[5] But this word, in
order to be capable of being understood as God's
conclusive self-expression and accepted in faith,
must fulfill the condition which Anselm set for
the idea of God: to be that "beyond which something greater cannot be thought". And God's self-
expression as absolute love *in himself* (and not first

Marie Dominique Chenu, *La théologie comme science au XIIIe
siècle* (Paris: J. Vrin, 1946).

[4] Cf. by the author, *Schau der Gestalt* (= *Herrlichkeit*, vol. 1,
2nd ed. [Einsiedeln: Johannes Verlag, 1968]; English ed.
The Glory of the Lord, vol. 1: *Seeing the Form* [Edinburgh and
San Francisco: T. & T. Clark and Ignatius Press, 1983]).

[5] Origen, *Comm. in Jo.*, vol. 5, 4–6.

in the relation of creation or of covenant), as he gives it in Jesus Christ's Incarnation, Passion and Resurrection, is "self-evidently" the fulfillment of this condition. But by virtue of this, every cognitive formulation of this self-demonstration of God is forced to refer beyond itself to absolute love, which not only factually but essentially "passes all understanding" (Eph 3:19). Each individual biblical theology remains, in relation to this center, a "figure" (an ideogram, or however one may translate the word in modern terms): "*Tout ce qui ne va point à la charité est figure. L'unique objet de l'Écriture est la charité*" (Pascal).[6] If this is true, then our train of thought divides as if automatically into three parts:

Where is the unity of the many Old Testament theologies?

Where is the unity of the many New Testament theologies?

Where is the unity of the many theologies in the Church?

[6] Blaise Pascal, *Pensées*, ed. Jacques Chevalier (Paris: Librairie generale française, 1962), no. 583.

2. The Unity of the Old Testament Theologies

The Old Testament supplies us with the classic model for the more general theological inquiry about the unity of the Bible. Two millenia of Christian theology have thought of the relationship between Old and New Testament in the schema of multi-faceted promise and single fulfillment, of many *typoi* and a single *antitypos*. If that is valid, then Pascal is once more correct: *"La figure a été faite sur la vérité, et la vérité a été reconnue sur la figure."*[7]

An essentially temporal religion, such as the Old Covenant, can *a priori* possess no purely supra-temporal truth perceptible in a comprehensive survey: Faith is following after the God who walks before us and directs us through time—without man's being able to know where the path leads. The situation of Abraham (Gen 12:1) and of the people in the desert cannot be left behind: God can issue new directives at any time. Therefore the Old Testament is not clearly to be interpreted and fixed according to its original situation (as Deuteronomy did with a certain preference,

[7] Ibid., no. 572.

though this origin was always put at "today", and as Martin Buber did when he measured everything later according to the original pure theocracy); nor is it clearly to be interpreted according to the path as such (such as the presently arriving word of the prophets, because the prophets themselves always point back to the beginnings, to keep Israel's faith alive); nor is it clearly to be determined according to the promise for the future (as the Apocalyptic writers would have liked to do), because the future events as such remain unrevealed and the images which indicate them may not be taken in the sense which mankind wants to give them (Jesus will die of this narrowing, which, practically, is disbelief: He does not correspond to the Jewish image); rather, it is to be interpreted in a sense which leaves everything open and which corresponds to Abraham's first obedience. The inner temporality of Israel's religion makes it impossible to fix one of the time-aspects as absolute.

Everything temporal and living "develops" somehow—changes from implicit to explicit. Let us single out a few examples at random: The "Ten Commandments" on the one hand formulate a single idea of the living God which clearly transcends the "religion of the Fathers"; on the other hand, they summarize the ethical statute of the twelve tribes to which the tribes subordinate themselves in obligation, giving up their individual statutes. But the Decalogue, which represents a transparent end-point, is once more transcended in the synthesis of Deuteronomy. The people, it says there, heard nothing more on Horeb than the "Ten Commandments"; seized by fear, they sent Moses ahead to receive Yahweh's further directives, for they wanted to obey them. The decisive thing which Moses heard and which he now imparts to the people as a testament at the end of his life is the *Shema*: the commandment to respond in love, with all human powers, to the God who elects out of groundless love— a commandment which is then also correctly grasped as the essence and synthesis of the Ten Commandments and all other directives from God. But the great prophets once more transcend this deuteronomic conception when they project the images of the origin into the future and make the possibility for the fulfillment of the Old Covenant as a whole dependent upon a conclusive act of salvation by God which will judge, purify and heal Israel and embody God's word in its heart.

That which is temporally living does not only "develop", but also comes again and again to end-points where something is fulfilled and must give way in its form, in order to make room for further development. The petals of the blossom must fall if the fruit is to ripen. Israel's history is full of such "cul-de-sacs", at whose end, each time, a "form" has come to completion which temporally can be brought no further in its perfection as image (*figure*, *typos*). Again, a few random examples: The original theocracy, as classically expressed by the words of Gideon (Jg 8:23), can no longer maintain itself at a particular point in time (in the Philistine war), and changes, among unclear ideological confrontations (many early and late voices speak at cross purposes in 1 Samuel 8), into a kingship which, after a fairly catastrophic history, does not justify and cleanse itself by the fact that, according to the books of Chronicles, an earthly king simply "sets himself on the throne of Yahweh" (1 Chron 28:5; 29:23; 2 Chron 9:18; 13:8).

One can also inquire when this nation composed of twelve tribes, this amphyctyony or confederacy, existed as the true partner of the covenant with God. Certainly not on Sinai; and at the point where it is exalted to a theological concept, at the time when Deuteronomy and Joshua were composed, it had long since ceased to be historical reality. As a mere ghost it lives on in the War Scroll of the Qumran, and an historical reflection does not fall upon it again until Jesus' choice of the Twelve as judges of the tribes of Israel.

The point of intersection where God's sphere and that of the people meet in the covenant is a highly sensitive, explosive spot. Moses stands there as mediator: With the words of God he descends to the people, and with the people's concerns he goes up to God. Prophets will carry on the first part of the role in particular. But the more evident it becomes how poorly the covenant is kept and realized, the more the mediator becomes the expiator as well: God's whipping-boy, who must vicariously bear the guilt of the people. This is seen as early as the writings of Hosea; thus also Moses of Deuteronomy, Isaiah with his "children", Jeremiah and Ezekiel, and at the end of the line the "servant of God" of the anonymous writer in the exilic period, who conclusively expresses the full idea which had slowly developed historically through the centuries. And an end and discontinuance were certainly never more abrupt than here; from the exile to Jesus the line is not continued, even though a faint echo of the powerful event may be heard now and then.

We know what doubtful elements accumulate around ritualism, around tabernacle, tent and temple. The idea behind all this is at hand and is so indispensable that even after the Exile, when the presence of the glory of God in the new temple seemed uncertain and became ever more doubtful, the cult of sacrifice—even bloody sacrifice—does not cease, in order to be delivered, as it were, as intact "figure" on the threshold of the New Covenant. "Without the spilling of blood, no forgiveness" (Heb 9:22). A gradual spiritualization of the liturgy was not intended in Israel, which was moving toward God's Incarnation, in which a questionable temple of stone was to be replaced by a Temple which is indubitable, spirit-filled, but based on Jesus' corporeality—the Church.

In the time after the exile everything becomes doubtful, even what is best and most necessary; it must show its inner fragility, its existence as merely a figure. The touching attempt of Judaism to continue the covenant, so shamefully broken before, through doubled diligence in painfully exact observance of the law, founders on the silence of the divine partner, of whom one literally does not know if he is cooperating or not. And yet the figure of "perfect obedience to the direction of God" was required.

How does it stand with "wisdom", which, after dubious political beginnings in the time of Solomon, deepens and becomes the area of "connecting links" within the Bible—first to the

Egyptian and old Oriental cultures, and then to Hellenism? Its figure was not dispensable, as is shown by the broad stratum of wisdom thought which runs through the whole New Testament; indeed, it becomes the foundation for the possibility of the gospel's being proclaimed in all the world. In itself it remains questionable and (in a temporal-historical religion like the Old Testament) almost a foreign body, as is shown in Alexandrian Judaism with Philo, who could not achieve the transposition of the Yahweh-religion into the Greek philosophy of religion.

In Daniel a few strokes of apocalyptic lightning had flashed through the dark sky and shown the form of a pre-existent Son of Man, to whom God entrusts the judgment. It is very problematical when an entire apocalyptic literature takes these lightning-flashes under its own management, ascends itself to the "places" reserved for God and establishes a previously unheard-of intercourse between heaven and earth; and yet one must ask whether the New Testament event would have had enough conceptual material to express itself without this dimension.

Everywhere we see figures which are either temporally ending or internally finite, figures which—and this is the decisive point—cannot be linked together into a total picture, even in projection to the future.

Certainly the human need for integration had to make the attempt to push the great symbols together, to make them overlap in part. And New Testament exegetes search with eagle eyes for the marks of such combinations in the late-judaic period shortly before Christ. The results are minimal. Although, for example, a certain expiatory function was assigned to the martyr, it did not occur to anyone to identify a martyr with Isaiah's servant of God. David's Messiah, Daniel's Son of Man, the promised Moses-like prophet (Dt 18:18), the perfect high priest, the servant of God, the temple itself, the Pascal lamb, the scapegoat, and the other sacrifices: None of all these coincided. Precisely the form's being approximated in time hinders its inner opening towards and communication with the other forms. *Tout est figure*.

And behind all individual figures the riddle of the origins remains—the open question between Abraham and Moses: God's one-sided promise to Abraham, to which he had to respond with boundless faith, and the covenant with the people, necessarily two-sided in some measure. For a great king who enters into a covenant with a vassal may act out of kingly grace to a great extent, yet in spite of this there is a mutual obligation. Indeed, the more gracious the great king proves himself, the more justly he expects the vassal's return. Faith and law—as Paul will show almost too vividly—stand in a tension which can scarcely be resolved.

The more deeply one considers the apories into which the Old Covenant runs and the more one realizes both their theological urgency and their insolubility, the more wonderful their solution in the New Covenant appears. For here alone the Old Covenant has its unity; in itself it cannot find unity. But in what way and under what conditions can Jesus Christ establish the unity of the Old Covenant?

3. The Transcendence of Jesus Christ

The evangelists provide the key when they attest— each in his own way—that the synthesis effected by Jesus became clear to them only after Easter and through Easter. This clearly means that Jesus did not spend his earthly life reconciling the contents of the Old Testament titles of majesty— indeed, that he probably never assumed these titles himself at all. He lived and fulfilled the will of the Father to the last: The titles and their contents, of themselves, fell to his share all together like portions of the spoil. He fulfilled his mission at a point which proves, in retrospect, to be the point toward which—in some unimaginable way!

—all figures of the Old Covenant converge. But this point could not possibly be found on the level of the figures, for the figures contradicted each other (on their own level)—at times diametrically. Only because Jesus transcends the figures and remains in a kingly freedom with regard to them do they fall to him as if incidentally—and yet centrally, insofar as they could come to belong to no one other than him.

The transcendence of his event is shown in the fact that a *breakthrough* is effected in his historical existence, which divides at once into a breakthrough upward, to God, and downward, to death and hell. Insofar as he is *Verbum-Caro*, God and man, he is at the same time the realized covenant and the solution to the riddle of tension between Abraham and Moses: He is the Word of the Father returning to God with the whole human "accomplishment", and the human accomplishment is precisely the "complete faith", pure obedience. From this, the double breakthrough becomes understandable.

Upward the image of God is supplemented in that God is not only the freely choosing Love in relation to Israel and, eschatologically, to humanity in general and the world; rather, God is Love in himself, namely absolute, that is, triune Love, which does not need man in order to possess an object of love. For if this idea were seriously entertained, man would without fail receive power over this God who needs him, and the path would go on irresistibly, either to Hegel (because man then surveys the depths of God: God only becomes truly God through the necessary unfolding of his capacities as a creator, through the creation of his vis-à-vis, in whose release and home-bringing he first discovers himself—who he, as God, is and what he, as God, can do) or to the *homme révolté*, who has already been achieved in Job and who has become for many moderns the shibboleth of the actual man, because man's freedom is made free to explore the weakness of God, and in this perverse way to search "the deep things of God" (1 Cor 2:10) or "the so-called 'deep secrets' of Satan" (Rev 2:24). Only the identity of freedom (of election) and love in God himself, only the mystery of the Trinity which God discloses to humanity in the making of the New and eternal Covenant in Christ, surpasses definitively and irrevocably God's self-revelation in the Old Covenant. This mystery is "*id, quo majus cogitari non potest*", but it is revealed not as doctrine but as active self-demonstration, for God loves the world so much "that he gave his only Son, that whoever believes in him may not die, but may have eternal life" (Jn 3:16).

In this sentence the opposite abyss is also open: the possible perishing of the creature gifted with freedom, and the "giving up" (giving up for lost) of the Son through the Father, in order, reaching below, to gather in the lost ones in death and hell. This breaking of the gates of hell did not exist in the Old Covenant by virtue of law: God's partner in the covenant is mortal man, and the extent of the covenant is mortal life. All apocalyptic or moralizing anticipations must factually "wait" (Heb 11:39 f.) for the *decensus Christi* in order to realize themselves in the event of Easter, rising with him (Mt 27:53).

Christ's new foundation, his Church, is the communication to mankind of the *pneuma*, interior to God, which is the location, consummation and testimony of the love between Father and Son. Henceforth the Church exists consciously, the unbelieving world unconsciously, within the trinitarian love, which proved itself to be the final thing, the *eschaton*, because in the midst of its opposite—in the "hell" of lost human freedom— it could be itself, as the Son's perfect obedience of love even in the realm of the dead.

In the New Testament, then, there is one single total truth, one single dogma, which at its center is christological, but in its immediate implications is trinitarian as well as soteriological, and, indeed,

soteriological (*decensus* and Resurrection) *as* trinitarian. In this the Christ-event not only fulfills
all the figures of the Old Covenant, but—as the
Apocalypse of God's final mystery—is *already and
forever ahead of* every possible world evolution and
all the "figurations" which could appear in it,
which is why Christianity does not have the least
thing to fear from any evolutionism.

This single "dogma" has unrolled once and
for all the absolute horizon for all the partial
views which the Old Testament had opened:
for faith (of Abraham), for good works (of Moses:
dividing his goods among the poor), for *gnosis*
(of the wisdom books) and for prophecy (of
the prophets). All this, on this Old and New
Testament level, is eschatologically "suspended",
superseded (1 Cor 13:1–3, 8–10) in the face of
the love of God which does not end. So far as
this love became apparent in its self-declaration
in Jesus Christ, every overtaking of this love
through *gnosis* is excluded: This particular will
never be transformed into something "universally
valid". But as far as in the fact of Jesus Christ
the "*id, quo majus cogitari non potest*" really becomes apparent, every positivism of revelation is
excluded, so that Paul rightly uses a dialectical
formula: "to understand the *agape* of Christ which

is beyond understanding" (Eph 3:19), and Anselm seconds him, no less dialectically: "*Rationabiliter comprehendit incomprehensibile esse.*"[8]

The love appearing in Christ is *God's* love, not ours (1 Jn 4:10). It is given to us so that we can answer God in this gift. But the act of letting oneself be given to, faith, comes before the response, the works, just as Abraham comes before Moses, and as the one-sidedness of the promise was the basis for the two-sidedness of the covenant. And yet the other aspect must also be stated (and this other aspect comes to light in the testing of Abraham at Moria): To believe in God and in his love means to accept, at once and always, the manner ("the law") of his love, to subordinate oneself to this manner and let one's life be determined by it. Real faith always contains love. Thus Romans 4 is always to be interpreted and made living in the light of Galatians 2:19–20. And only then, in this horizon in which the absolute love of God, which entered for my sake into death and abandonment, becomes clear to me, do I understand how completely my being is directed and judged [*gerichtet*] by this love: What sin and

[8] Anselm, *Monologion* no. 64, in *Opera Omnia*, ed. F. S. Schmitt (Stuttgart: F. Frommann Verlag, 1968), vol. 1, 75, line 11 ff.

failure are in their depths, I experience in the horizon of forgiveness. Before this "abyss of the riches and the wisdom and the knowledge" of God (Rom 11:33), however, our second question opens:

4. The Unity of the New Testament Theologies

For it is clear to begin with that this abyss, this "fullness" (*pleroma*), which on the one hand lets the "fullness of God" dwell in Christ (Col 2:9) and on the other hand lets the Church be filled with his fullness (Eph 1:23) and lets creation as a whole find its fullness in him (Col 1:19), cannot be expressed through a one-dimensional, surveyable theology. While the multiplicity of Old Testament theologies was conditioned above all by their temporality, the multiplicity of New Testament theologies is caused by the "bodily" presence of the divine fullness within history. To proclaim the absolute event in the kerygma required the theological work of translation into considered, coherent words: the kerygma—and the whole New Testament is kerygma, in the broader sense—is a translation of the *logos-sarx* back into *logos-rēma*.

The tensions which are to be theologically overcome appear greater than those in the Old

Testament. For, first of all, the proportion between the Old and the New Testament is at issue. This proportion is imperfectly, only essentially described through categories like Promise and Fulfillment, while the mode of existence changes fundamentally: from a being "before God" (or God pitching his tent "among us") to a being "in God" (or God's dwelling "in us" or our dwelling in Christ, in the Spirit, in the openness to the Father). But in the essential aspect, too, it must be shown what is meant when Christ is called the "true high priest", the "true Paschal lamb", the "true servant of God" and so forth. The word "true" is defined each time through the particular figure as well as through its being surpassed. The figures and their mutual tensions, then, are not simply brought along behind us; they are present and exert their influence as aspects which are preserved and included. Finally, the figure of Jesus Christ which draws everything else together in itself, in his birth, life, Passion, death and Resurrection, is anything but surveyable. At the center of this figure gapes the deepest, logically unsurveyable, abyss: the sinking into the eternal night of Godforsakenness with the muteness of the dead Word of God on Holy Saturday, and a wholly new beginning, which certainly fulfills everything but does not continue from anywhere, being instead a new creation altogether. The hiatus between Good Friday and Easter cannot be bridged by any chronology; its explosive power is stronger than any worldly time; and precisely this hiatus is also the "place" at which Christology originally proves to be trinitarian and soteriological. Trinity becomes originally evident in the opposition of "my will" and "thy will" in Gethsemane and in the cry of abandonment on the Cross. And it is precisely at this point that the soteriological *decensus* occurs. Out of this timeless hiatus of Holy Saturday, New Testament theology is born.

This theology can never be a single one. Leaving all other questions aside and selecting only one: *How* is the "time" of the Church qualitatively determined through its relationship to this (non-) time of Christ? In what sense can a time of the Church be spoken of here, since the Church herself arises centrally out of this hiatus? But where—one might ask—will it then be "placed" within the time of Christ? It must always be considered first that Godforsakenness has no time (because it is final and not temporary, and no more hope exists in it); that Holy Saturday has no time, because the dead person who is to experience the fate of those separated from God cannot be animated by the "divine virtues"; that the Resurrection, finally, can only be described as an instant and not as time, or at most as the (eschatological) boundary between the world's time and God's time.

The Church in her self-understanding—which she needs for her kerygma—cannot situate herself precisely in regard to this mystery of time. Perhaps Mark wrote his Gospel in orientation toward the experience of the Resurrection, which at the same time might have been understood as the experience of the second coming. Perhaps Matthew had in mind rather the dimension of the transcending of the old (Old Testament) time through the fulfillment of Christ, and from this fulfillment he moves, with the good news, toward his fulfillment (in the *parousia*). For Luke, God's all-embracing time of salvation extends, not univocally, but in deepening stages: from the Old to the New Testament, from the event of life and death to its self-interpretation in light of the Resurrected one, and from the trinitarian occurrence of the Ascension to the pouring out of the divine Spirit on the Church. But all three, in addition, return to the simultaneity of the faithful with the earthly Lord moving toward the Cross: "From the Cross of Christ" becomes "with Jesus to the Cross". The two balance each other in John, where crucifixion and glorification coincide, and all differentiations of time integrate themselves into the presence of Jesus, who is always "*the*

Resurrection" and "*the* (made–present, trinitarian) Life", and only thus "the Way". Thus the circle nearly comes round again to Mark. But for Paul, the Exalted one who encountered him remains essentially the Crucified one with whom he, Paul, wishes to be crucified, but at the same time resurrected; all questions of chronological time (nearer or more distant expectation of the *parousia*) pale completely in the face of this paradox.

What is the point of these all–too–brief reminders? The point is to show that it is impossible for the Church to define precisely the relationship of her time to the time of Christ. Indeed, precisely the most important point remains inexplicable—her standing on this side or the other side of the great hiatus. She must stand on both sides and let the hiatus out of which she arises be above and below her. She is buried with Christ and risen with him. She dwells with him in heaven yet waits for him on earth. Much too little is expressed by the simple word "eschatological", for this lifting up of time into the eternal and the invasions of eternity into time have so many perspectives that the word establishes, at best, a broad parameter. Every hagiographer stands at a different point within it and receives a different perspective. And yet each is given the task of opening up, in his fragment, a view of the whole. And because all have this whole in view and are attempting to express it, their theologies can never really be separated from one another. From each to each, *cross-ties* run back and forth, and their roots weave together. For Paul also says that only all together will be able to measure the breadth and length, the height and depth. Indeed, this will be possible precisely in virtue of their union in love, in which they should be "firmly rooted and grounded" in order to understand the four dimensions of that love of Christ which passes all understanding (Eph 3:17 ff.).

Here we reach the point at which the horizon of ecumenical discussion first appears. Precisely that transcendence of Jesus Christ which manifests its power a first time in the unification of the Old Testament is now also that which renders the Church possible in her innermost essence: as "being in Christ", as the area or organism (*soma*) put forth and directed by him (as head) which manifests— from him, and toward him—the fullness of Christ (Eph 1:23). This fullness is pure grace, which we all can only receive (Jn 1:14, 16), and this grace is identical with the trinitarian love given to us in Christ, which presents itself in the Church's unity of love. Thus the "paranetic" sections of the Pauline letters, which admonish in every form to love within the Church, are nothing other than

the existential exercise of the "dogmatic" section:
That which *is*, *should* also be. Where someone
offends against love, Christ in his Body is "crucified
and mocked anew" (Heb 6:6), and instead of
works of the Spirit, those of the flesh are performed, among which are "rivalries, dissensions
and factions" (Gal 5:20; 1 Cor 3:3; 11:18–19; Phil
2:3–4). *Ubi peccata, ibi schismata* (Origen). *Peccatum*,
in relation to the unity of the Church, is that
delusion which—to go back to our initial image of
the kaleidoscope—because of a deceptive effect of
the mirror, rounds off the essentially fragmentary
nature of an individual standpoint (characterized
by a special charism) into a totality, which then
naturally has no room for other views.

Paul forms the grandest model for the avoidance
of this delusion in the twenty-first chapter of Acts,
where he—coming with the whole of the Gentile-
Christian community to Jerusalem—meets James.
Not a word is said about the reception of the gifts,
and the joy which is spoken of at first appears to be
quickly stifled in the following speech by the
brother of the Lord. He tells Paul that "rumors"
are going around about him among the Jews con-
verted in Palestine—that he "teaches the Jews
who live among the Gentiles to abandon Moses,
to give up the circumcision of their children and

to renounce their customs". From James' standpoint, this freedom—not only regarding the Gen-
tile Christians, but also regarding the Jewish
Christians—appears to exceed the agreements
reached at the Council of Apostles. Above all he
fears the practical consequences: namely, that the
thousands of Jews gathered for the feast will
become agitated. Therefore he lays before Paul a
plan he has thought out and asks him—actually in
the tone of command: "do as we tell you"—to
show himself in the Temple with other Jewish
Christians who have taken an Old Testament vow
upon themselves and to pay for them. "In that
way, everyone will know that there is nothing in
what they have been told about you, but that you
follow the law yourself with due observance"
(Acts 21:17–24). James probably does not know
what he expects of Paul here: nothing less than the
abandonment of that which forms the kernel of
the letters to the Galatians and Romans and which
Paul has often called "my Gospel". Whoever may
have been meant by the curses at the beginning of
the letter to the Galatians, we hear nothing more
of that sort here, nor any "I cannot do otherwise,
God help me, Amen", but only a silent following
of the given "advice" (v. 25), which then promptly
goes awry in its effect: Sent from the brothers to

the "Jews", Paul is taken prisoner by them and, like his Master, passed on to the Gentiles for sentencing. All that is important for us now is Paul's almost incomprehensible self-surpassing, for which there is only *one* interpretation: The unity and love of the Church are more important to him in this breaking-test than his own standpoint, more important even than the particular mission entrusted to him personally by Christ. For every ecclesiastical mission comes forth from God "according to the analogy of faith" within "the one body whose many members we are" (Rom 12:6, 4). Every mission is enclosed by the "bond of perfection", the divine love in Christ, and this love which breaks forth from God's innermost being (*splanchna oiktirmou*) manifests itself chiefly as "kindness, humility, meekness, patience" and mutual forgiveness, because the Lord has forgiven all of us (Col 3:12–14).[9] It is precisely at this

[9] One should read what Clement of Rome, in reference to this quotation, has to say to the schism-happy Corinthians about the bond of perfection: 1 Clem 49:1–5. Let no one object that the above interpretation of Acts 21 is a secondary, Lucan dramatization and does not prevail against the primary, Pauline statements (on faith and justification). Faith, for Paul, remains inseparable from love—it is love's obedient acknowledgment—and love is always love of God together with love of neighbor in the unity of the Church. 1 Corinthians 8 shows that faith in the one true God (8:6) is love of God ("If

point that the Pauline doctrine of justification receives its final consecration. Paul commends it to the Lord of the Church, who may dispose of it now and in the future according to his free judgment; and the Lord himself will prepare its triumphal procession down through the millenia.

5. The Unity of Theologies in the Church

On the basis of this model we may dare to address the formidable problem of the theologies in the Church. By this is meant, not the harmless differences among schools within the Catholic Church, but those theologies which have operated practically to divide the Church, and to a great extent conceive of themselves in that light theo-

---

anyone loves God, that man is known by him" [8:3], and is thus in the truth) as well as love for the weak brother, love which gives up its right and its better insight: ". . . that brother for whom Christ died! When you sin thus against your brothers and wound their weak consciences, you are sinning against Christ" (8:11 f.). Cf. Romans 15:1–5: "Christ did not please himself: 'The reproaches they uttered against you fell on me'." As Christ's obedience brings him abuse, so the loving preference of ecclesiastical unity "in the spirit of Christ" brings contempt to the "strong ones" in the Church: They could not see how to assert their mature insight successfully!

retically as well. After everything that has been said we can first of all—from the highest observatory, so to speak—venture the statement that a Christian truth which divides the Church is an internal contradiction, an "impossible possibility", as Karl Barth would say; for Christian truth *per definitionem* can only be unifying for the Church. If we descend from this highest observatory, there exists in the Church of sinners the perpetual danger of seduction and therefore the perpetual duty of mutual exhortation (*paraklesis*) to remain with Christ's truth; the same word can mean a beseeching, imploring request. Almost all the letters in the New Testament are, in their basic sense, this *paraklesis*: to hold oneself in the center of the truth from which alone the whole truth can be seen and possessed. Everything which deserves to be called reform again and again in the epochs of Church history has been active, effective exhortation to turn back from the periphery to the center.

The center is Christ, of whom the entire Holy Scripture speaks: the entire Scripture, quantitatively—not a selection of writings out of the canon—and qualitatively—not a selection of viewpoints, especially when this selection excludes other available viewpoints. This does not prevent certain great lines of strength from running through the whole; indeed, these are to be heeded if one wishes to extract a theological structure of order out of the *corpus* of Scripture. And yet we should be on our guard against setting up a "canon within a canon", according to which other things can simply be condemned. The tendency toward the "canon within a canon" is the tendency toward the substitution of *gnosis* for *agape* as the highest value. Even when a primary element can be determined as opposed to a secondary—as Abraham's faith, for example, is primary as opposed to the Mosaic Law and "works"—the question always remains whether the primary does not already contain the secondary (that is the idea of James 2:20 ff.) in order to be able to be itself at all, whether the second is perhaps only the explication of the first and whether one therefore does not commit *hairesis* if one wants the first without the second, or places the two only in a dialectical relationship to one another. Here the *terrible simplificateurs* have an easy task and the laugh on their side in theological matters, while those for whom the integration of the secondary elements is important along with the hierarchy of viewpoints easily incur the verdict of lacking radicalism. Karl Barth's invectives against the "Catholic And" can be important and even indispensable as earnest brotherly exhortation— particularly when they protest against something secondary being put in the place of something primary—but they can also prejudice, too quickly and unnecessarily, a necessary integration.

A word about the Evangelical-Catholic controversy in general is appropriate here. The present ecumenical dialogue, although it is frequently understood as a cooperative search for Christian truth in focus on the mutual Lord, is understood also as a radical reduction to the allegedly "essential", along with the elimination of all dispensable additions which disturb the understanding. It is clear that the Catholic partner will draw the shorter straw under these conditions, for the Reformation already lightened the ship of all its alleged "ballast" four hundred fifty years ago, and today, in the face of the events within the Catholic Church, it speaks, not without satisfaction, of a "need to catch up". Because Protestantism has assumed the most diverse and contradictory forms in the course of its history— strict orthodoxy, pietism in the old and new Schleiermacherian style, and finally liberalism to the extent of a "theology after the death of God" —the ecumenical agreement can also proceed on the most different levels on account of such throwing out of ballast; and the abandonment of Catholic goods (allegedly those of the "Counter-Reformation" above all) can then be carried on more or less summarily. Against all this, attention must be drawn to the following point: Just as biblical theology is highly complex and cannot be reduced to a "systematic" denominator, so ecclesiastical theology, which has only to mirror biblical theology and make it ready for the proclamation of the gospel, is not constructed of short-sighted formulas and hastily set up as a "system", but requires an obedient consideration of all aspects, as well as the capacity not to disregard what is supplementary (to the fullness of Christ!) within the necessary gradation. Evangelical and Anglican movements of our time are intensively concerned with winning back such goods of integration— think of Taizé and Grandchamps, of the Anglican cloister movement, of the new appropriation of Mariology, the Holy Mass as a sacrifice, the ecclesiastical teaching authority and the literally interpreted life of following Christ in the evangelical counsels—while in the Catholic camp it is contemporary to throw all these things, like cheap trifles, into the rubbish. This is certainly not obedience to the Word of God; even less so for the Catholic, as he must be aware that it is not an individual devout man or researcher, nor any one modern tendency or sect—comparable to the Corinthian parties—but the Church as a whole who is the steward and overseer of all Holy Scripture, whose final canon she alone, under the guidance of the Holy Spirit, has determined.

With this mention of the Holy Spirit, indication

is also given, in conclusion, of the necessity of *prayer* for the understanding of revelation. Someone who no longer prays has certainly already missed the common ground, that which ecumenism is concerned with. The common focus on the Lord of the Church, who is also the total content of Scripture, is synonymous with common petition for the Spirit of the Lord. In this common prayer, the approaches are opened to us in common to the common truth, which will be a truth of the highest, most mysterious fullness, and not one of simplification and surveyability. If we are all docile before God (Jn 6:45), then Christ can be our common teacher (Mt 23:8); and then, like the Kingdom of God, the unity of the Church is "near", "even at the door" (Mk 13:29).

THE UNITY OF OUR LIVES

It is said that the dying, in their last moments, often see their whole lives as if compressed into a picture—perhaps like a film which rolls by once more with monstrous, almost timeless swiftness, or like a landscape through which they have wandered slowly on foot and now see again from an airplane. It seems to me that such a synopsis must be something frightful, something which forces the dying person to evaluate that which he has lived through in many years and now sees as a whole as senseless, almost perverse. What was the significance of all the little steps, the daily tasks, usually so meaningless, which filled the life now spent? Except for a very few, they were put together out of very sparse content and a power, going beyond this and pressing further, which we may call hope. Let us not discuss the so-called Paradise of first childhood; it may be that in the first awakening of consciousness, the human senses—eyes, ears, touch and taste—are beset by wonderful experiences whose novelty fills the whole psychic space and scarcely leaves room for disappointment. But how quickly these Paradises are lost—perceptible once more, at the most, in moments of intensive play. The irksome, without whose performance man is not educated, claims its place: One must always be doing something which one would rather not do. The child must go to school, willing or not; it hopes for recess, for Sunday, for the vacation. The student hopes for the time of professional employment after his examinations; the apprentice hopes to become a master. But how thin, how threadbare, the fulfillments remain. Consider the faces of the masses rolling to work at eight o'clock in the morning or after lunch; everyone must earn, sit through their time, and be at the disposal, with a friendly face, of customers or supervisors. In the evenings when they are tired they can arrange their so-called leisure time: with radio and television, with automobile trips over the weekend, or, when the sun shines, with splashing in a swimming pool. There are the family joys: They are purchased with countless sacrifices and renunciations. And there is the remarkable thought that all of my sparse and generally so unbelievably disappointing action has some meaning in relation to the human future: that in the end my vanishingly

small contribution makes a difference in the immense sum of the whole—a difference, to be sure,
which scarcely anyone will think about after my
death, yet which nonetheless was there and went
into the reckoning, which would not have worked
out quite so easily without me if it should ever
work out at all. . . .

But we want to narrow down once more the
large field of questions which opens before us. Let
us leave the problem of human progress (I suspect
that precisely this phrase does not occur to the
dying man who is surveying his life once more);
let us leave even the beautiful, touching hope that
my trifling involvement in the human reckoning
claims a post which cannot be wholly forgotten.
(But not everyone can console themselves with
this thought: What edifying contribution do the
children starving in Biafra offer? What contribution was made by the millions of gassed Jews?
or by the chronically ill, the insane, those who
have admittedly bungled and neglected their existence, the unwanted, aborted children? and who
knows how many other insoluble question marks
which are crushed by the steam-rollers of the
belief in progress, but rise again uninjured behind
them.)

Let us leave all that, and look only at any

average minute of our daily existence. None of
them is fulfilled in itself. Each one, to be endured,
needs that power which thrusts forward, hope—
that anticipation of the future—so that the Now,
which always melts away, can be affirmed. Between that which I actually am or could be or
would like or ought to be, and that which I
factually live, do, think, judge or experience just
now, there gapes an abyss which I can only bridge
by virtue of this advance of hope. I never exist
completely in my actions and circumstances. I
am joyful, but the joy does not penetrate to the
last core of my self; there is room for fear, for
boredom, for something else which is new, opposite, and which will probably—no, certainly—
dissolve today's joy. Perhaps that is the worst
thing for our dying man who sees his life march
past: how almost everything has become obsolete.
Friendships and love relationships which seemed
eternal at the moment are shattered and written
off, names are crossed out of the address book as
obsolete; what tasted good to us before is now
insipid, works of art which we once admired say
nothing to us today; we smile or sneer now at the
tears we have shed. The experiences are lifted
away from our self, almost without hurting it;
perhaps it still hangs on to this one or that, but it
already has so much practice at letting things go

(not to say, at betrayal) that in all likelihood it will be distrustful of this hanging-on and will almost painlessly complete the final operation which cuts away even these threads to the past which still cling to it.

But then it will be consistent if a final attitude defines our whole life: caution, holding back, reserve, not getting in too deep, keeping avenues of escape open. Here I must call to mind a few verses of a poet who is neglected today, but who is unique in his experience of existence and in the magic of his expression:

> . . . Alas, whom are we able,
> then, to use? Not angels, not men,
> and the shrewd beasts already notice
> that we are not very reliably at home
> in the interpreted world. There remains
> to us perhaps
> some tree on the slope, which every day we
> would see again; there remains to us the
> street from yesterday,
> and the warped faithfulness of a habit
> that liked being with us, so it stayed and
> did not go.
>
> . . . Everything was commission.
> But do you master it? Were you not always
> still distracted by expectation, as if

everything predicted a lover to you? . . .
Lovers, you, you who are satisfied in each
  other,
I ask you about us. You grasp each other.
  Do you have proofs?
      . . . (You) promise yourselves eternity
  almost
from the embrace. And yet, when you sur-
  vive the fright of the first
glances and the longing at the window,
and the first walk together, *one* time through
  the garden:
lovers, *are* you still so, then? When each to
  the other
raises the mouth and joins—: drink upon
  drink:
O how strangely, then, the action eludes
  the drinker.
Were you not astonished, on Attic statues,
  by the caution
of human gestures? Were not love and parting
laid so lightly on the shoulders, as if they
  were made
of other stuff than with us?

What Rilke describes here and in many other
places in his work flows into the resignation of
caution. Is it not the same thing which all the great

Eastern religions have always offered as the final wisdom of life: not to let oneself be taken into the spinning wheel, so that one does not remain hanging on fate, so that one preserves a freedom in the midst of all love and all suffering, a passionlessness in everything which creates passion, a calmness which from the start—with Saint-Exupéry, for example—surveys the whole mechanism of existence from the icy, glorious and levelling height of an airplane, or in the strange and yet closely related and easily recognized transformation of our youth, a flower-existence which opposes the dead senselessness of our technical daily operation and its equally senseless (because empty) "principle Hope" with something somehow organic and living: existence as a beautiful game, like the flowers of the grass blown here and there in the wind—in the wind of fate, certainly, which many young people clearly sense is a wind of ruin. Flower, because otherwise everything remains empty, because it is too late for anything else.

Humanity today, if we except the remnant of Christianity, seems to be divided into two camps as far as its world view is concerned, camps which cut across the fronts of East and West. One is the dogmatic camp, and the dogma is this: The meaning of existence is the progress of the species and, at that, the self-guided, self-made technical progress as is being inculcated with great emphasis in America. I quote several sentences out of a lecture by Herbert Lüthy that appeared recently in *Monat*:

> If the writing of history is to have a meaning, so runs the postulate (that, namely, of the American ideologists), if it is to be something other than a confusing recollection of confused happenings, it must be the historical presentation of the only meaningful progress, the only one of which it is certain that it did and does exist—of the progress of the technical-scientific civilization and not of the drama of those who perished on the path of this progress or were crushed by it. That is briefly the program which the General Director of UNESCO, René Maheu, has set for the encyclopedic, super-national and apolitical Universal History of Humanity, which is financed by the Organization, and which its prominent co-worker Charles Morazé presented in his "Logique de l'histoire". . . . Nearly ten years ago Charles P. Snow, in his famous *Cambridge Rede Lecture* on "the two cultures", put the historical-literary-humanistic disciplines in the dock as hotbeds of reactionism, if not of nihilism, because they do not, like the natural scientists and technicians, have "the future in their bones" but the past, and because they occupy themselves with stale conflicts, ideologies and tables of values while the scientific culture

bridges conflicts and ideologies: For, he says, when two scientists, regardless of their antecedents or observance, discuss their science, they speak the same language—"and that is what culture means."

What is presented here is dogmatic faith in the strictest sense of the word because it is not verified either in the individual's experience of existence or in that which he finds by way of meaning for existence in present humanity. Certainly this horrendous technical progress exists: But from the acknowledgment of this fact to its equation with the meaning of the human being, and thus of being in general, is a huge step, or let us rather say a cleft which is unbridgeable by thinking reason, across which only a dogmatic faith can leap. For anyone who does not want to subscribe to this coercion of dogma there remains the other, ancient, oriental solution: freedom from the whole, caution, serenity. Do not almost all the great authors of our time tend basically in this direction, in connection with which the particular variety of this world view is not at all important? It can be but need not be Zen, or any kind of Buddhism; there are also variants of *gnosis*, even into the lived-out backgrounds of our new depth-psychology, our structuralism and our cybernetics. . . .

But we are asking about the unity of our lives. Is this ancient eastern, finally world-wide and omnipresent religion of serenity and dis-illusionment capable of resolving it? Does it not rather offer us a unity of meaning which lies *beyond* the meager fragments of meaning in our daily life—in something which continues identical, which does not enter into any of the differences of existence itself, which neither affirms and justifies today's joy and the love of this person nor earnestly condemns and judges tomorrow's pain and the betrayal of love? a meaning, then, which does not contain in itself the unity of our unique earthly life because it does not collect the sequence of fragments in order to shape the totality which we always seek and never find, but instead throws the whole varied collection into a wastebasket to make room for the One, the unity, which always was beyond all else, and, unconcerned with all else, always will be? Even if this second way frees us from the dogmatic coercion of the eastern-western belief in progress, its freedom gives us no genuine solution to our question.

We really had to reach out this far in order to make this statement evident: Only that God who became man in Jesus Christ, who took all human guilt and unfulfillment with him onto the Cross and into Godforsakenness, and who as man was *resurrected* and placed in the divine-eternal life by God the Father—only he is able to unify our existence. For now Christianity appears in its absolute solitude and incomparability. This consists in the fact that here alone, through the hope of our resurrection in Christ, everything unfulfilled in our individual moments of life receives a hidden fulfillment, and in the same stroke the loose pearls of our individual hours and days are strung together on a strong thread; that our time, considered both horizontally and vertically, receives —if we only desire it—a true unity, enduring in the presence of God's existence above time.

How does this come about? Basically through the fact that for the Christian, and for him alone, God is love—essentially, in himself, and therefore also for the world created by him. "The Father loves you", says Jesus (Jn 16:27)—not from the inaccessible height of Allah or even of Yahweh, where an abyss which cannot be spanned gapes between our perishable selves and his imperishability ("All mankind is grass. . . . Though the grass withers and the flower wilts, the word of our God stands forever", Is 40:6 ff.). Rather it is precisely this word of God remaining in eternity which has become flesh, man and time and mortality and joy and suffering and life and death; and, as such a man, God's eternity has lived among us, or, as it says more precisely, pitched his tent among us, just as God's glory on Sinai required its own tent long ago in the nomad camp of the Israelites. This Incarnation event is understood as the last and highest work of God the Father's love: "God so loved the world that he gave his only Son, that whoever believes in him may not die but may have eternal life" (Jn 3:16). And so that we do not think this was an idea peculiar to John, we will cite Paul as well: "Is it possible that he who did not spare his own Son but handed him over for the sake of us all will not grant us all things besides?" (Rom 8:32). And in this "all things", certainly, lies unity, and thus the meaning of our lives. But in this "not spared", "handed over", there hides a last and, we might say, scarcely credible mystery for the Christian understanding, a mystery which is almost too beautiful to be true, and yet has been held as true by the Christian Church for two millenia. Paul says it thus: "God sent his Son in the likeness of sinful flesh as a sin offering, thereby condemning sin in the flesh [of this man]" (Rom 8:3). Then in this man he also condemned my sin, everything that I did wrong during the long ages of my existence, my false paths, my blind alleys, my infidelities against my fellow man, against myself, and most profoundly against

God—in the end he condemns all these discrepancies between me and my action, behavior and experience. This whole sum and burden of the guilt of my existence is taken over, borne and settled— when and through whom? Not through a stroke of the pen in heaven, for I would know nothing of such a thing; and if I did have some information about it, I would not be so certain that I could trust it completely, for better or for worse, and could assure my existence of a complete salvation. Nor was it accomplished through a fellow man alone, for how could he not be in exactly the same state as I, just as much in need of healing and therefore incapable of taking over my entire calamity and bringing it to recovery? Where and through whom, then? Only through him who is God's real, divine Word to us all and to me in particular, and who, sent and sacrificed as a man—but a wholly unique man—for the sake of our sins, is able to bear them, both as a whole and in particular.

This is the first, most basic Christian fact, on which everything stands or falls. There is no complicated machinery, but rather, so to speak, the minimal beginning so that the sought-after unity can come into man's life—a minimal beginning, to be sure, which in itself is an unsurpassable, inconceivable maximum: God's love for us, for me, to the extreme—to foolishness, as Paul says, and what lover would not gladly take on the appearance and reputation of a fool if his love really depended on it? If this first fact is valid, it unfolds itself for us into three truths.

The first is that there is someone in whom the elements of our existence, which are cast forth, lost, wasted in the emptiness of time and the impersonal space, are brought together—in their complete deficiency, their powerlessness and their failure. If we are really loved by the eternal Father, then the hairs of our head are numbered by him, our needs are known, our mistakes are regarded with kindness and—through this tireless love which makes up God's essence—compensated for. And when he lets us do penance for many things, because children sometimes do not learn any other way, these penances which he lays upon us are one more expression of his love. "The Father loves you." With him, then, is the place where the flowing brooks of our existence, all appearances to the contrary, collect and run into a single stream. Now Jesus' word becomes clear: "Do not lay up for yourselves an earthly treasure. Moths and rust corrode; thieves break in and steal." Whoever collects on earth has a rapacious attitude, whether his treasures are material or spiritual, and this attitude is the contrary to love;

therefore it always loses what it means to hold.
Under the hand, in the very clutch of the rapacious
arm, the treasure is consumed and stolen away.
"Make it your practice instead to store up heavenly
treasure, which neither moth nor rust corrode
nor thieves break in and steal." And now the
enigmatic conclusion: "Remember, where your
treasure is, there your heart is also" (Mt 6:19 ff.).
If it is with you yourself, then your treasure will
pass away together with you and your heart, as
everything temporal vanishes. But if you throw
your heart to God, then you want to keep nothing
at all for yourself; you give him the care of your
treasure, your unity, and he protects it for you in
his eternity. There you will find your life one day,
in its true underlying unity, which never appears
on earth.

This hope of finding the rubbish heap which
every human life finally represents to be a well-
constructed, inhabitable building is certainly based,
from the Christian perspective, on God's grace,
which knows how to assist human deficiency
everywhere, fills in the gaps of our unrealized
being, interprets and takes up the whole accumu-
lation as a formed word, and supplements, out of
the wealth of the divine life, that which we with
our human life are incapable of making full. We
call this grace. And grace is not only a matter of

being looked upon graciously from above; it is also the pulsing of divine life through our half-empty arteries. But we only achieve the certainty of such grace and the justification of such hope through Christ's Cross, in which "he cancelled the bond that stood against us with all its claims" (Col 2:14). That means that God's work on us is not simply performed from the heavenly heights; it is work from within, laborious detail work at closest proximity. We are not summarily judged and then, as guilty persons unable to pay, let go out of grace and mercy. Instead there is someone present who collects piece by piece everything which has been wasted, frittered away and squandered; someone who pays for us, as the Samaritan pays for the wounded man who was robbed and cannot pay for himself—and does not pay meagerly, but with an advance deposit and a surplus: "If you have further expenses", he says to the innkeeper who takes the wounded man in, "I will cover them for you when I return".

Naturally we are not looking here into God's mysterious reckonings. How is the suffering of God's Son related to God's mercy and justice? How is it sufficient that he, as one individual, should pay for all? How impenetrable must his suffering be, and how abundant, that a surplus still remains? "Twelve baskets full". And the hardest fact to grasp is that it is the Father's love which lets the Son suffer for us. It is no harsh, obdurate justice, which insists on the settlement of debts, but simple—if incomprehensible—love, which introduces itself to us and makes itself credible precisely in this manner, if we only had the grace to notice how it wants to be understood and accepted by us. God's mysteries become almost more dense with the unveiling of his love.

But in spite of this we may record an initial result: If we are Christians, that is, if we understand God as love—and he wants to be understood as that love—then we have confidence and certainty, this wholly unique and wild hope which contradicts all experience of existence, that our existence will one day be given to us as unity—not laboriously patched together, nor as a new, strange form to which our earthly fragments could contribute nothing, but precisely as our form, in which we really encounter ourselves for the first time and are finally that which we had always wanted to be.

But now we come to the second, most important point in our whole consideration. Where will I meet this healed, whole self that I will be? From the Christian perspective there is a single answer: in the Thou, the Thou of God the Father, who loves me and has the healed, whole image of me from all eternity. But he has it (as we are told) in his Son, who is called simply "the beloved" (Eph 1:5 f.); and in order that no deception may arise here, that nothing may be represented outwardly as beautiful which in reality is inwardly ugly and nothing as eternal and unified which is perishable and shattered, God the Father lays his own and his Son's Spirit in our heart, so that we may call him "Abba", Papa. God's Spirit, not our own, gives us the totality, and it lies in God's Son, not in us ourselves; but there, with the guarantee of perfect authenticity and trustworthiness, we are the perfected work for God the Father, which he had in his mind from the beginning. It is in the Thou, then, that we find our I.

We know something about this basic law through love between human persons. In the love of the mother the child finds its consciousness and its self. In the mother's heart it finds the support to firm its groping, fragile existence into a form. In the Thou, wife and husband are told and shown who he is, who she is, in truth. Love is creative for the fellow man; it produces an image of him with which the beloved would not have credited himself, and when love is genuine and faithful it gives him the power to come closer to this image or make himself like it. He does not want to disappoint; he wants to show himself grateful that someone takes him so seriously and expects so much of him. Such a thing succeeds in a fragmentary way on earth, in mirror and likeness. It receives its full truth in Christianity. A Christian never has his unity within himself; nor does he in any way seek it in himself. He does not collect himself around his own center, but rather wholly elsewhere. "The life I live now is not my own; Christ is living in me. I still live my human life, but it is a life of faith in the Son of God, who loved me and gave himself for me" (Gal 2:20). And now, please, attention: That he loved me and gave himself for me is an already accomplished fact, outside my psyche and psychology. It is not the subjective impression which releases this fact—accomplished or perhaps only imagined—in my psyche, and not the power of my faith which connects me to my unity in Christ beyond my personal wreckage. Such a psychologizing of faith would kill the innermost nerve of Christianity, and the I would again be alone with itself—with itself and its psychological faith and its psychological hope. But what Paul thinks and says with all clarity is something wholly different: that my failing, guilty I, before all my knowledge and action, is included by Christ in his Cross and death; that precisely there, in that event, it is settled and put behind me, and my real, actual,

believed-in and hoped-for I lives *in him* and comes
to me from him.

Now all at once we understand in what a profound sense we can speak about a Christ of the
future, and that we may await the experience of
Christmas year by year, indeed, day by day. He is
coming for me, the one in whom I *will* be what I
should be and would like to be. I am not yet so,
but live meanwhile in hopeful faith; that is, I shift
the central point, the main emphasis of my self
out of my ephemeral, decaying present into his
promised future, guaranteed as certain through
his Cross and Resurrection. This future is my
homeland. "We eagerly await the coming of our
Savior, the Lord Jesus Christ. He will give a new
form to this lowly body of ours and remake it
according to the pattern of his glorified body, by
his power to subject everything to himself" (Phil
3:21). It is consoling for us that Christianity, with
its miracle of faith, presents itself as the perfection
of a truth which we already know about from our
human world and which we can recognize as the
most profound and fruitful precept of life: that a
self can in the end be found and sheltered only in a
loving Thou. God became man so that this law,
which is understandable to us—perhaps the most
understandable of all the laws of life—should turn
for us into the definitive law of being, explaining

and satisfying everything. In Christian faith alone, then—to say it once more—lies the single sufficient explanation for human existence.

Let us say a third and final thing. Only he who escapes from the prison of his self is free. Because the Christian lives in faith in the God-man "who loved me and gave himself for me", he is the freest of men. He is not only free for an earthly duty, for an involvement, a mission, a bond in marriage and community. These are also freedoms, but only relative ones. The Christian is absolutely and finally free. For he and only he has the certainty that he is eternally loved, and with almighty power. Everything earthly can be destroyed for him, every form of his life can dissolve into shapelessness: He remains unshaken in his certainty that for God he is someone unified, even someone individual and indispensable. This is what the first Christians demonstrated when they accepted martyrdom for their faith with such power: not out of fanaticism, not out of escapism, but out of the certainty that man, in the end, finds his unity in Christ. The astonishing words of Ignatius of Antioch summarize this consciousness: "It is better for me to die for Jesus Christ than to be king over the ends of the earth. I seek him who died for us, I desire him who rose for our sakes. . . .

Brothers, do not keep me from life. . . . Let me receive pure light! Arrived there, I will be a man" (Rom 6:1–2). Until then he considers himself a nobody (Eph 3:1), a miscarriage (Rom 9:2), "but through mercy I will be a somebody, when I attain to God." So speaks this early martyr, who presses full of impatience toward his actual incarnation. We will not be allowed to press in this way, for we have been given an earthly task. But in anticipation of the incarnation of our death God's Incarnation lies in our mortal life, to bestow upon it form and unity from the very beginning in faith, hope and love. And because God's love comes to us, we may wait in patience until it takes us to itself in fulfillment. It is the same both here and beyond and, precisely in its coming to us, has shown itself for that which it is, and as what only the Christian knows it to be.

In all the foregoing we have spoken personally: out of the situation of a dying man who, looking over his life, is always completely lonely. But it is not difficult to expand this perspective to the great I which is formed by humanity as a whole, whose millenia-long path of life, on the day of its certain death, will also appear to it as an immense rubbish-heap—when this great I looks back, not on the cultural and technical achievements which it will perhaps have accomplished, but on the millions of little I's out of whose hopes, disappointments and despairs it was and will be composed. And the final great I of humanity, which must come before God's judgment seat, will not be more than the sum and integration of these small I's—unless the miracle should occur that on top of this formless "body" should be set a "*head*" from which the formless and futile mass receives, beyond all hope, a structure, a content and a justifying meaning, so that all our common and so breathlessly pursued work, all our common and so unequivocal failure, is made, from this sublime position—"as if through fire" (1 Cor 3:15)—into an organism which deserves, as God's perfected kingdom, to be spread before him as a dwelling place (1 Cor 15:24).

ONLY IF

The Japanese doll: Open it, and you find a second one inside—similar, smaller. Open this one, and you find the third. Keep going until you come to the tiny last one, indivisible. Then, my child, you have nothing but halves, and now show your skill: Put all the divided ones back together so that finally only the one doll stands there, filled with the contents of all the rest. (And don't forget that the smallest one is indivisible.)

1. Immemorial, irretrievably expanding universe (why does it exist?), self-ruminating monster for which death and annihilation are inner, indifferent law—and at the other end tiny earth, and on her, tiniest man, unconditionally finite, mortal, but claiming to be and to become the lord of this monster. He cannot despise the monster as that which is purely quantitative, cannot immerse himself, fleeing, in his own spirituality in order to exalt himself above matter. In spite of this he knows that he will never come to terms with the

135

blind, over-mighty forces; even if his species accomplished the taming after millions of years, it
would still be a species vanquished through end-
less times, and who can make up for its losses: the
unthinkable suffering and despair, the senseless,
horrible destruction of beings whose purpose for
existence had to be contained in the narrow circle
of birth and death? The species which storms
toward the future (but is vanquished in advance)
does not have time to be bothered with its decaying past. Who will gather up the futilities and
despairs? Who has so much compassion that he
does not simply watch sympathetically (from his
own freedom from suffering which he has perhaps
achieved), nor wrathfully plans for redress (for
the next time), but in solidarity bears the responsibility for all that cries to heaven, bears it in
com-passion (which must cry even more fright-
fully to heaven)?

Only if the same one who has the monster
world on his conscience, who possessed the incomprehensible power and the frightful courage
to let this monster loose, *only if* this one not only
shares in the most terrible anguish but surpasses
it by laying hold of it from below (for only God
can know what it means to be truly forsaken
by God), *only if* that Maximum coincides with this
Minimum (both beyond our comprehension)—

not in indifference, but in such a way that absolute
power becomes one with absolute powerlessness
in sheltering compassion, thus *only if* God is triune:
if the same God is Father and creator of the cosmos
and man, and if he is the Son who gathers all
forsakenness into himself in the Godforsakenness
on the Cross, and if he is the love between the
two, and if the love stretched and extended to the
uttermost is a single Spirit, Spirit of the Father
and the Son, Spirit of strength and weakness,
Spirit of the same love: only then do I receive
a key which makes the meaning of being credible
and endurable to me—without my comprehending
either the meaning or being.

For if (in religious absorption) we strive away
out of the world and suffering, then world and
suffering are only an appearance (which is surely
false). And if (trusting in evolution) we seek
only to build a better future, we betray our dead
and are forced to surrender our dignity as persons
into pure anonymity. Between "religion" and
"utopianism", only a Christian-trinitarian basis of
meaning can give a reason for the world and
reconcile it with itself and its appearance.

2. Man is torn in two between the smallest
circle, to which he is assigned by virtue of his
sexuality—the Thou of love: wife and children,

the importance of the family, which must be cared for—and the largest circle, humanity as a whole, to which he inevitably inclines by virtue of his nature, with which he knows himself ever more closely bound through technology, and from whose destiny he cannot disassociate himself. But between the extremes there is no continuous mediation. The circle of friendship and acquaintances is limited; the more one seeks to expand it, the looser the relationships become, and the more one threatens to neglect the duties in the most intimate circle. That one has a social calling and cooperates vaguely toward the common good (and lets oneself be paid for it) cannot console in the end; and the vague humane attitude, the Samaritan willingness to help, which occasionally becomes active when someone crushed by fate is lying in the street before us, can neither appease our bad conscience (one would have to do much more, but one does not know how!) nor strengthen our good conscience (I do, in the end, what I can, and one cannot ask more of me).

Only if the same one—it must be a single person!—brings together in his existence the two irreconcilable sides of existence, the individual and the social, in such a way that he not only does justice to both for himself, but can also justify, through himself, all the others who do not succeed in doing so, *only if* this one, who hung before on the Cross as the Godforsaken, can really embody the two ends of humanity, by virtue of his unity with the Father and the Spirit: the man fallen among thieves and the Samaritan, everyone who is starving, thirsting, sent into exile, freezing in nakedness, sick and imprisoned in loneliness, and everyone who gives food and drink, every hospitable person, everyone who gives clothing and shelter; only if our failing, always and unavoidably guilty existence were to be drawn into such a unity, and in it were not only outwardly "pronounced righteous" (that would avail nothing), but were inwardly empowered to a totality which it cannot accomplish of itself—only then would hope exist for man to perfect himself (beyond himself and yet in himself) in such a way that he would not have to shatter upon the dialectical structure of his existence, but instead could take the tribulation of being human upon himself with joy and gratitude. For if the Godforsaken one on the Cross is the whole, effective compassion of God with his world, and if the guilt of all is borne by this one so that the bond of guilt against the world has been torn up, if faith in the love of God, so mighty in the powerlessness of love, is an unconditionally obedient surrender to the law of this love, then the incomprehensible can happen: my longing to do better than I can, beyond my insufficiency and failure, is taken up into the synthesis of the Cross. This synthesis justifies me, indeed, out of the grace of love and without my agency, but thereby it gains the right to claim me according to a transcendent law of love, to interpret me according to its meaning and to exploit me for its purposes, until I can no longer situate myself because I am wholly dispossessed in the service of the one and the same, who encounters me as the same person in the exclusivity of my I-Thou relationships as well as in the anonymity of every relationship to those nearest and those most distant.

But this is only possible if that one is not simply a man like me, like us all—for otherwise how could he help us out of our dialectic of guilt?—but the divine Son as man, in whom the whole love of the Creator and Father embraces us all as powerful-powerless compassion. If God's Trinity was the first key to the meaning of existence, Christology is the second.

3. The individual could perhaps content himself to be thus taken into service in God's work in humanity, which transcends him and in which he is absorbed, bearing anonymous fruit not in himself but in the whole, the "mystical body" of God,

which is to become the world some day. But
if he could so forget himself, might he also deny
himself a definite, final being-loved? A fellow
human being has said Thou to me, and with this
Thou has definitely meant me, chosen me and
"made me eternal". Can I detach myself gently
and say to him: Our love cannot be final and
definite, it remains conditional within the boundaries of death? Certainly death, which cuts across
all bonds, proves the transience of many of them;
but how terrible if it should unmask all love,
which most deeply desires and promises eternity,
as illusion or a biological trick.

Only if the unprecedented and most improbable
of all breakthroughs results—through the iron
curtain of death—only then can love be that
which it purports to be according to its essence.
Only if God, who is eternal, free love, enters into a
covenant with mortal, guilty man, in which he
promises to deliver him over the boundary of
death onto the side of God (the Old Covenant),
and if he fulfills this promise at the end of his Son's
Passion and this finite, temporal and ephemeral
life as a whole is "resurrected" and sheltered in
the incorruptible life of God, *only if* the moment
which promises eternity does not deceive in the
end, if existence is finally to be relied upon because
its supporting base is eternal love itself, which is

stronger than death, *only if*, in Christ's Resurrection, his apparently futile suffering for the world is taken over, in the form of the stigmata, into the glory of the Father—and with the stigmata, the calluses of his carpenter's hands and all the spiritual wounds which were notched into his soul through earthly experience—if the whole unabridged earthly existence, with its futility and together with the effort of all humanity, is transfigured and justified with God: only then does God not need to be ashamed of his creation, the plan of which can after all work out in no other way than this. If man is created spiritual and free, then he can lose himself in final death, away from God; but if God is triune and if he can carry out in himself, in the unity of his Spirit, the tension between Father in heaven and Son as man in Cross and death, then death and lostness become a form of his almighty love: Out of Trinity and Christology follows the truth of Resurrection or Redemption, without which there would be no solution to the human paradox of love. But all this is not deduced from the apories of existence (which would produce only a *gnosis*); instead, it is read from the appearance of God's love in Christ, which is not necessitated and cannot be dissolved into any *gnosis*. The proof of this is that without Christ (as man and eternal Son of God together), in pre-Christian terms the synthesis presented here remains unthinkable, while in post-Christian terms it necessarily vanishes again ("trinity" for Hegel is only a formal law of being, "Christology" becomes an idea with accidental historical occasion, and "resurrection" is dismissed as the presumptuous claim of the ephemeral individual).

4. The disciples of Christ, who on Easter recognized the Crucified one, the carpenter's son and their teacher and master in the Resurrected one, saw the synthesis completed in their experience: Jesus is the Christ, that is, the fullness of the promises (which could and even had to be given under different ciphers: Messiah, king, prophet, high priest, heavenly Son of Man, sacrifice and Paschal lamb, sin-bearing Servant of God and so forth). In this synthesis, which is the core of "dogmatics", all the principal aspects of faith are implicit: the pre-existence of the Son (thus his membership in the sphere of God, and so the core of the doctrine of the Trinity), soteriology (the Resurrection itself was a proof for the "*pro nobis*" of the Passion), but also ecclesiology, whose space was marked out by its origin—Israel as God's partner-nation—and its goal—the world redeemed through Cross and Resurrection, toward which the new "people" of those who have recognized and believed in God's action in Christ is under way.

Only if the new partner-people was grounded in Abraham's unconditional surrender of faith (to follow blindly where God leads), and in this faith accepted God's definitive action in Christ—who, however, was not the second Abraham in relation to God, but was rather the new and genuine Adam, the universal man—*only if* the fidelity to the faithful God which was unconditionally required of the old nation (and was even then represented by the symbol of marital fidelity between man and woman) is also incarnated in the Incarnation of the Son of God, if through God's grace of incarnation a new Eve stepped to the side of the new Adam, only then could the innermost essence of the new nation be described: The old mystery of "man and woman as one flesh" became the basis and the image for the new mystery of God and man as one flesh, Christ and Church as one body. This central mystery becomes fully concrete—as concrete as the Word of God's becoming flesh—through Mariology. The prefiguring Old Testament cases in which barren women give birth as proof of God's power are surpassed, with innermost consistency and in direct continuation of the Old Covenant, by the Spirit's overshadowing the Virgin Mary, whose total, Abraham-like faith becomes, with highest theological precision, the womb for the Incarnation of the promised one and thus falls itself under the law of incarnation: Virginity, as spiritual exclusivity of faithfulness to God, embodies itself (as bodily motherhood) in the embodiment of the Word of God. Together with the new Adam must come the new Eve—through him ("pre-redeemed" in his grace) and at the same time as a condition for him (through her faith and her female womb). An isolated man, even though he be God, is not a whole human being; he needs the "helpmate". The new people is a Christian one only if it helps, as *ecclesia*, to prepare the ever new Incarnation of God, and lets itself be formed ever anew through God's Spirit into the Body of Christ. Whoever skips steps or pulls stones out of the wall at this point, possibly the most dense aspect of Catholic dogma, fails in the integration; he will not accommodate the logic of the Old Testament in the New, and the New will not open itself for him into the mystery of the universal man; his understanding of "eschatology" will not rest on the whole breadth of the original basis of creation— the inter-human I-Thou in general, and especially the sexual; and the entire resulting historicity of the human race and fellowship will always stop somewhere, unintegrated and competing (as the so-called horizontal next to the so-called vertical). For *only if* God truly becomes man—and that happens only if the unity of people and bride, of ecclesiology and Mariology, is taken seriously—do God's plans begin to be fulfilled: his plans to take mankind and the world to himself in such a way that they also come wholly to themselves.

5. The new people distinguishes itself from the old in that it is included in the mystery of the flesh, as "body" and as "bride". Both concepts are used in a real sense, though also—compared with the natural level—supereminently. The bodily Christ, who is God's perfect partner on earth, should be "incorporated" by the faithful, which naturally can only mean that they must be incorporated into his real bodiliness, in order thus to become his members, his brothers, sisters and mothers.

Only if the most real historical body of Christ, which in its historical existence, its Passion and Resurrection, contains the compassion of God with his world, is communicated to the faithful in its reality—only on the condition, then, that there is the mystery of the Eucharist—do we truly participate in the God-man's fate. Here the analogy of food and drink becomes the significant basis in creation, along with the analogy of sex, and within the perimeter of this analogy are drawn the analogies of other acts and situations to serve as signs of the Christian's distinctive unity of destiny and commission with Christ. But above all man is essentially speech, spiritual-physical communication of self. Christ as a whole is God's speech to us: eternal word, which speaks through its total existence and therefore necessarily through its human word; so that the divine communication occurring through its total existence will be understandable to us, it is always put into speech. *Only if* (along with the Eucharist) the communication which has occurred in Christ is put into words that are forever binding, that is, into Holy Scripture, does the Incarnation become complete for the Church. This word is delivered up to her as something spiritually living but at the same time fixed and irrevocable, for nourishment and passing on as word of prayer (to be given back to God), as word of preaching (to be sowed out in the world), as ecclesiastical word of love and above all as word of (sacramental) forgiveness, gifted with the corporeality and the spiritual power of its origin. Communion in the one Body of Christ and communion in his Word and Spirit belong most closely together, as close as the body and spirit (word) of a living man. But if the form of the Church (as people-body-bride) is a social one, then the unity within it can be expressed

and supported only through an ecclesiastical authority; and such an authority was present from the
beginning. *Only if* this ecclesiastical authority is
not only composed in a human-organizational
way, but is also christologically based, can it
help to protect the christological unity of the
ecclesiastical Body of Christ. In its mind, and in
the minds of all those obeying it, must be the absolute obedience to Christ, who himself achieved
absolute obedience to the Father on the Cross, in
atonement for the world's disobedience. In the
"chief shepherd's" commission to the Church's
shepherds to feed Christ's flocks, there lies the
duty of one's own example as well as the duty of
that kind of demand for obedience which (looking
strictly toward Christ's lordship) leads to absolute
obedience to Christ. This is possible *only if* those
who have been baptized understand that they are
baptized into Christ's death—that is, if they acknowledge the highest rule of Christ's existence,
his obedience to the Father, as their own rule of
life to be ever more deeply realized, and if they
understand the spirit of Christian maturity as the
spirit which makes its decisions out of the complete
indifference of faith's obedience to God. He is
mature who, through the Church's education, is
drawn out of open and hidden selfishness into

a participation in the accomplishment—in every situation—of the obedience of the Body to the Head, or of the "lowly handmaid" to the Lord and Bridegroom.

6. The synthesis "Jesus is the Christ" (and that means in truth God's Son and "the Word in the beginning with God") is the gratuitous, real unity, given by God and not to be postulated by any philosophy, between Creator and creature; therefore, for man, it is the indissoluble unity of his relationship to God and his relationship to his fellow man and the world. That God dies for man in freedom is certainly true; but in this, God's death is the most proportionate expression of the eternal life of his love. The pronouncement "God is dead" is only true within the pronouncement: God's death is the final proof of his over-living, triune love.

Scripture speaks of our having died with Christ *only if* it confirms our resurrection and our hidden life in heaven in the same sentence. And we may regard ourselves as having died with him, "continually given over to the power of death", "at all times bearing Jesus' death-agony in our body", only when we offer up our living existence in gratitude to the Lord of our new life, and to our fellow man. Christian existence becomes credible *only if* we "are like the dying, and behold we live, deprived of everything, yet possessing everything and enriching everyone". This will be completed in living fashion *only if* we do not turn our backs on the love of God which redeems us in order to attend only to our neighbor, but instead always keep the absolute love, "who loved me and gave himself for me", before us as the final horizon—in commemorative, thankful praise—and fulfill our Christian and worldly attention to fellow man and vocation before and toward this horizon. Since we ourselves (and the whole world) exist only as embraced between the Creator God and the Redeemer on the Cross, in the place of the Holy Spirit who is and bears witness to the unity of the two, we do not need either to dislocate ourselves artificially when we turn to God (as if we then lost sight of the world) nor imagine that we are set up as a shuttle service between a worldless God and a godless world. God is become man. But let us not act more stupid than we are and triumphantly proclaim: Thus he has stopped being God and is now nothing more than the fellow man. Faith in God as triune love, and proof of this faith through active love of neighbor, are rather in Christian terms a completely self-evident, unproblematical, thoroughly transparent unity. *Only if* I have prayed and have been gifted anew with God's love can I enter on the difficult adventure of fellowship, without lusting after power and without anxious instincts for flight. And *only if* I love my neighbor for the love of God can I show him and give to him what he really needs: not only a finite and failing Thou, but in the midst of it an "imperishable treasure which the moths do not eat". *Only if* I ask for God's almighty power can I endure an unbearable human situation to the end, instead of running away: The point where no human word has any more worth, where human love only embitters and estranges more profoundly, is precisely where the mystery of the Cross begins to shine. Therefore a Christian who consecrates himself without reservation to the mystery of crucified love (in vows of human-divine poverty, ecclesial-marian virginity and ecclesial-christological obedience) is in the end the man who is most fruitful for the world, if he carries out the vows in earnest. He gives not only things and deeds; he gives himself to the world which is to be redeemed together with God, undivided, once for all time.

7. The abysses of the Father's absolute power and the absolute powerlessness of the Son, mediated by the absolute freedom of the Holy Spirit, are so open that they guarantee every possible space for

the immeasurably unfolding being of the world. *Only if* God guarantees the room of omnipotence, all–forgivingness and all–freedom does the evolution of the world not press out into emptiness, so that it finds even in itself no more meaning as a point of support. And *only if* Christian faith perceives itself as faith in this incomprehensibly Ever–Greater of the divine dimension (and in no way as faith in an event and stage of thought which can be overtaken by history and evolution) does it know itself; only then can it understand its everlasting, never weakened actuality and make it understandable to others; only then is it able rightly to consider every competition from other religions, world views and models of the future as wholly irrelevant. Christian faith does not believe in just anything; the content, which is always true (proven through the "smallest, indivisible doll", the indissoluble synthesis: "Jesus Christ"), is always in advance of every possible (conceivable or inconceivable) evolution of the world. It is not as if the Christian were raised above the exertion of work in the world, or as if he had patent solutions for it. The dimension of death and resurrection, the eschatological dimension, does not lie in the area of that which evolves. The frame which the Christian religion offers is once and for all too big for every possible growth of the earthly picture. And yet the growth of the picture is not a matter of indifference to the frame: Creation sighs for perfection, and the divine Spirit also sighs for perfection out of the depths of the human heart and out of all the beings subject to decay. God, in power and powerlessness, is most profoundly interested in this perfection. Therefore the Christian also, with every bit of his Christianity as well as his humanity, is involved with an interest that is actually divine in the perfection of the world. *Only then* does he belong to the new people of God, which is always on the way from Cross and Resurrection, confession and Eucharist, to the brothers, to tell them of God and of his interests.[1]

---

[1] Naturally this little essay is only one of a hundred other possible ways of integration (and to that extent the analogy of the doll limps). The decisive Christian truths all mutually imply each other, because they are after all only aspects of the One—*unus necessarius!*—who is himself the truth.